Patrick McAlister, Bishop of Down and Connor, 1886–95

Patrick McAlister

Bishop of Down and Connor
1886–95

Ambrose Macaulay

FOUR COURTS PRESS

This book was set in 11 on 15 point Galliard by
Mark Heslington, Scarborough, North Yorkshire for
FOUR COURTS PRESS
7 Malpas Street, Dublin 8, Ireland
Email: info@four-courts-press.ie
and in North America for
FOUR COURTS PRESS
c/o ISBS, 920 N.E. 58th Avenue, Suite 300, Portland, OR 97213.

© Ambrose Macaulay and Four Courts Press 2006

A catalogue record for this title
is available from the British Library.

ISBN (10-digit) 1–85182–997–0
(13-digit) 978–1–85182–997–2

All rights reserved. No part of this publication may be reproduced,
stored in or introduced into a retrieval system, or transmitted,
in any form or by any means (electronic, mechanical,
photocopying, recording or otherwise), without the
prior written permission of both the copyright
owner and publisher of this book.

Printed in Great Britain
by MPG Books Ltd, Bodmin, Cornwall.

Contents

Illustrations

Preface

PATRICK MCALISTER was bishop of Down and Connor for nine years. Before his appointment his entire career had been spent working unostentatiously in parishes in the diocese. As a seminarian he had not won academic distinction and his only involvement with education after ordination was in his capacity as a manager of national schools.

He did not take a prominent part in the meetings of the Irish hierarchy and his name would have been little known outside his own diocese. His work can best be described as a continuation and consolidation of that of his immediate predecessor, Patrick Dorrian. Dorrian had made provision for the increasing Catholic population of Belfast by equipping the town with churches and schools and by bringing in religious orders dedicated to education or to the care of the sick, the poor and the homeless. Throughout the diocese he had encouraged his clergy to enlarge and repair churches, and, where necessary, to build new ones. Each parish was also required to update the local national schools or provide new buildings.

In other, less pleasant ways McAlister had also to continue Dorrian's task of coping with riots and sectarian disturbances, especially in Belfast. Shortly after his appointment he was faced with worse violence than that ever encountered by Dorrian. The Home Rule Bill of 1886 was defeated in parliament but not before bitter opposition to it had led to serious disturbances which cost the lives of thirty-two people and left many others injured, displaced, or deprived of the means of earning their living. Seven years later the second Home Rule Bill also provoked sectarian disturbances but on a much lesser scale. McAlister was deeply worried by these religious antagonisms and animosities and devoted much time and energy to attempts to calm the passions that led to such painful and destructive consequences.

Some 60,000 Catholics, more than a third of the population of the diocese, lived in Belfast and its immediate suburbs. The electoral system which obtained during McAlister's episcopate effectively excluded them from membership of the corporation. Partly as a consequence of this and partly because of prevailing sectarian attitudes, their representation on the boards of management and, indeed, of the work-force of public bodies was minuscule. Catholic distrust of those who held a monopoly of power was correspondingly large.

Another political problem of McAlister's episcopate, and one which he shared with all his fellow bishops, was the response to the determination of Charles Stewart Parnell to remain leader of the Irish Parliamentary Party after the exposure of his relationship with Katharine O'Shea led to her divorce by her husband. He endorsed his colleagues' rejection of Parnell's leadership, and fought obstinately and acrimoniously against the Parnellites in the nationalist political organization in Belfast. Riled by the support given by the local nationalist paper, the *Morning News*, to Parnell, he founded the *Irish News* in opposition to its Parnellism, and in defence of Catholic views. Here too he followed the policy of his predecessor in establishing a Catholic press – and with more lasting results.

But with less than happy results for the pastoral care of some of his people, he also pursued his predecessor's policy of limiting the spiritual activities of the Passionist community in Belfast. He maintained Dorrian's hostility to the only male religious order in the diocese with stubborn and unyielding determination. And though regarded by the *Northern Whig*, which served a mainly Liberal Unionist readership, as retiring and pacific by temperament, he could be, as his participation in these political and religious struggles showed, resolute and intransigent.

I am grateful to all those who have helped in the preparation of this book. For permission to use archival material I should like to acknowledge my indebtedness to Cardinal Josef Tomko, former prefect of the Congregation for the Evangelization of Peoples; to Cardinal Mejía, former archivist and librarian of the Holy Roman Church; to Cardinal Connell, former archbishop of Dublin; to Bishop Patrick Walsh of Down and Connor; to Bishop Colm O'Reilly of Ardagh and Clonmacnois; to the late Bishop James McLoughlin of Galway; to Bishop John Fleming of Killala and Monsignor John Hanly, former rectors of the Pontifical Irish College, Rome; to Monsignor Liam Bergin, the present rector; to Fr Martin Coffey, provincial of the Passionist province of St Patrick; and to Dr Cahal Dallat.

I wish to thank the librarians and staffs at the British Library Newspaper Library, the Belfast Public Library and the Public Record Office of Northern Ireland. For their kindness in reading my typescript and giving me much helpful advice, I am happy to thank Fr Joseph Gunn, Dr Brian Trainor, Professor Brian Walker, Dr Margaret O'Callaghan, Dr Eamon Phoenix and Dr Patrick Maume. I should also like to express my gratitude to Dr Michael Adams and his staff at Four Courts Press. Finally I should like to express my gratitude to the Bank of Ireland for its very generous sponsorship of this publication.

Belfast, 1 February 2006

Abbreviations

ACDA   Ardagh and Clonmacnois Diocesan Archives

ADA   Armagh Diocesan Archives

AICR   Archives of the Pontifical Irish College, Rome

APF   Archives of the Congregation for the Evangelization of Peoples
       (formerly *de Propaganda Fide*)

ASV   Vatican Archives

BNL   *Belfast News-Letter*

DCDA   Down and Connor Diocesan Archives

DDA   Dublin Diocesan Archives

FJ   *Freeman's Journal*

GDA   Galway Diocesan Archives

IC   *Irish Catholic*

IN   *Irish News*

MN   *Morning News*

NW   *Northern Whig*

PCA   Passionist Central Archives, Dublin

PMG   *Pall Mall Gazette*

PRONI Public Record Office of Northern Ireland

UOb.   *Ulster Observer*

UI   *United Ireland*

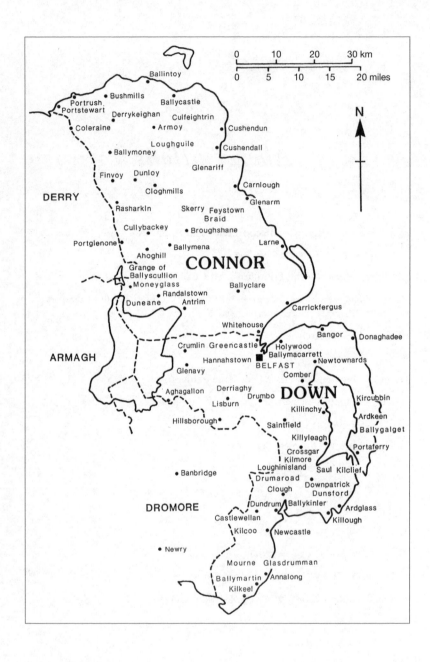

0   10   20   30 km

0   5   10   15   20 miles

N

Ballintoy

Bushmills
Portrush
Portstewart
Derrykeighan
Ballycastle
Culfeightrin
Coleraine
Armoy
Cushendun
Loughguile
Cushendall
Ballymoney
Glenariff
Finvoy
Dunloy
Cloghmills
Carnlough
DERRY
Glenarm
Rasharkin
Skerry Feystown
Braid
Cullybackey
Broughshane
Portglenone
Ballymena
Larne
Ahoghill
Grange of
Ballyscullion
CONNOR
Moneyglass
Ballyclare
Randalstown
Duneane
Antrim
Carrickfergus
Whitehouse
ARMAGH
Bangor
Donaghadee
Crumlin Greencastle
Holywood
Ballymacarrett
Hannahstown
Newtownards
Glenavy
BELFAST
Comber
Derriaghy
Aghagallon
Drumbo
DOWN
Kircubbin
Lisburn
Killinchy
Ardkeen
Hillsborough
Saintfield
Ballygalget
Killyleagh
Portaferry
Crossgar
Kilmore
Loughinisland
Saul Kilclief
Banbridge
Drumaroad
Clough
Downpatrick
Dunsford
Dundrum
Ballykinler
Ardglass
DROMORE
Castlewellan
Killough
Kilcoo
Newcastle
Newry
Mourne
Glasdrumman
Ballymartin
Annalong
Kilkeel

Chapter One

From Bonecastle to Ballycastle

THE BARONY OF Lecale, according to the *Irish News* in its
obituary for Bishop Patrick McAlister, though but a small
portion of the diocese of Down and Connor, had probably done
more for religion than all the other parts of the diocese put
together.[1] Whether or not one accepts this inflated claim, which
by its very nature defies verification, it is undoubtedly true that
the barony provided many priests for the diocese. Of these,
three had served as bishops from 1825 to 1885, and if the
neighbouring parish of Loughinisland in the barony of
Kinnelarty were included, the Downpatrick area could be said to
have supplied Down and Connor with its bishops for almost the
entire nineteenth century.

Patrick McAlister, the fourth bishop in succession to hail from
Lecale, was born in the townland of Bonecastle on 12 April
1826. He was the second son in a family of six children of John
McAlister and his wife, Mary Kelly. John, a tenant farmer, held
fifty acres from the estate of Percival Maxwell, at Bonecastle,
about three miles from Downpatrick. The rather unattractive
and inelegant name of Bonecastle derives from the Irish *Badhan
Caistil* which means a rampart.

After his course at the local national school, Patrick transferred to the classical school in Downpatrick which had been

1 IN, 27 Mar. 1895.

13

founded and conducted for many years by the Revd James Neilson, the Presbyterian minister of the town, and which had been attended by his three predecessors in the see of Down and Connor. In 1846 he moved to St Malachy's College. Founded in 1833 as a boarding and day school, and as a junior seminary for the training of aspirants to the priesthood, tuition in St Malachy's was geared to the study of the classics which was a particular requirement for courses in theology in a senior semi-nary. Entrants to St Patrick's College, Maynooth could sit the examinations at various levels. In the autumn of 1849 McAlister successfully competed for entry into the Logic class, being adjudged to have attained a sufficient level of knowledge of the classics to be exempted from following the humanity and rhet-oric courses. After a year's study of philosophy he began the three year cycle of theological studies. He did not achieve any special distinction in the academic field and was forced by the needs of his diocese to make do with two rather than three years of theology.

McAlister was ordained priest by Joseph Whelan, the former bishop of Bombay, who frequently officiated on behalf of Archbishop Cullen, in the Carmelite Church, Clarendon Street, Dublin, on 18 September 1852. Two months later he was appointed to a curacy in Ballymena where he served until his transfer in April 1854 to Kircubbin. But during that time he was withdrawn for three months to replace the parish priest of Glenravel whose concentration on building a new church in the Braid involved frequent absences from the parish. From October 1856 to May 1858 he was a curate in Ahoghill, but was again withdrawn to take charge of Ballymoney parish from October 1856 to March 1857 pending the arrival of the parish priest. In 1858 he moved to the parish of Holywood and Ballymacarrett, of which he took charge for a time in the absence of the administrator and which he left to spend brief periods in Saul, Ballymena and Glenravel before leaving it permanently on 2 September 1862 to become parish priest of Ballycastle.[2]

McAlister's entrustment with the temporary administration of Glenravel and Ballymoney indicated the enjoyment of his superior's confidence and his transfer to Ballycastle as pastor at the age of thirty-six confirmed this view. The ancient parish of Ramoan, which had been separated from Armoy in 1825, had, according to the census of 1834, a Catholic population of 1,710. It was served by two churches: one in Ballycastle, which had been built in 1795 and enlarged in 1838 and one at Glenshesk, four miles distant from the town, which had been erected in 1827 and which McAlister renovated in 1863. Rathlin Island did not then form part of the parish.

By 1888, a diocesan census, which was much more carefully and thoroughly taken than that of 1834, revealed that the population of Ballycastle had fallen to 1,043. Throughout McAlister's pastorate it probably fluctuated between 1,100 and 1,200. The parish was therefore moderately sized and compact, and could be satisfactorily managed by one priest. From 1862 to 1869 McAlister did not have the assistance of a curate, but from 1869 to 1886 the diocese had sufficient clergy to be able to afford him the services of one. The parish, however, being very poor, was scarcely able to provide a basic income for two priests.[3]

The parish priest's commitment to the building of a new church brought about the appointment of the first curate. The old church which was too small and cramped and would have required extensive repairs was situated in an unattractive and inconvenient part of the town. McAlister was fortunate to find a generous response from the landlord to his request for a site. Not only did Mrs Amy Keats Boyd, a Protestant, make him a gift of five acres affording a commanding and imposing view of

2 O'Laverty, *Down and Connor*, v, 622–3.   3 McAlister to Kirby, 16 Apr. 1886, AICR.

the town and countryside but she also added a generous donation of £50 to the building fund. McAlister published the letter
he received from the landlord's agent which enclosed the gift
and in which he had been assured that 'Mrs Boyd has been actu-
ated by no other motive than one of common justice to her
Roman Catholic tenants' and wished that 'all her tenants, irrespective of creed, should receive from her the consideration due
to them'. In his own letter he praised Mrs Boyd's generous and
munificent contribution and remarked that the liberal sentiments experienced in the appended letter did 'honour to Mrs
Boyd and to her worthy and benevolent son-in-law, and will, no
doubt, be read with much pleasure by the tenants of the
Ballycastle estate'.[4]

The church was designed by the Revd Jeremiah MacAuley,
who was then a curate in Cushendall. He had been trained as an
architect before studying for the priesthood, and had designed
St Peter's Church in Belfast, the largest in the diocese. The style
chosen was that of a simplified Gothic, which was then being
used extensively throughout Ireland and the design made provision for a seating capacity of 650. The foundation stone was
laid on 7 June 1870 and the completed church was blessed and
opened by Bishop Patrick Dorrian of Down and Connor on 9
August 1874. George Conroy, the bishop of Ardagh, preached
the special sermon and the collection taken up on that occasion
amounted to £530. The total cost of the church (excluding the
spire which was added later) was £4,000. To defray these
expenses McAlister had begged widely throughout the diocese.

With the completion of the church McAlister turned his
attention to the educational needs of the Catholic children. In
1839 one of his predecessors, Charles Hendron, with a group of
parishioners and an equal number of Protestants had applied to
the national board of education for aid for a school on Ramoan

4 O'Laverty, *Down and Connor,* iv, 432.

Glebe. They envisaged an enrolment of 75 pupils (50 boys and 25 girls) and were granted assistance on that basis.[5] As the national schools became more denominational McAlister's immediate predecessor, James McGlennon, established a new school in the grounds beside his church in 1853 and successfully applied for grants towards the salary of the teachers and supply of books for the children. The full enrolment totalled 107 (60 boys and 47 girls) with an average attendance of 92 (52 boys and 40 girls). W.H. Biedermann, the rector of Ramoan parish and chancellor of the diocese of Connor in the established church, queried whether the location of the building conformed with the rules of the national board, but the Revd Samuel Lyle, the local Presbyterian minister, raised no objection, though he would have preferred a more suitable site.[6]

With the foundation of the new church in 1874 the old building was no longer required for religious services. McAlister decided to use it as a school. In 1875 he had it divided into three sections for boys, girls and infants. This entailed further expense on the parish and, in an attempt to reduce it, Bishop Dorrian preached a charity sermon in Ballycastle. Emphasizing the great importance placed by the church on the apostolate of education, he stressed the obligations of local communities to their children. On that occasion £143 was collected.

In 1880 the last basic need of the parish was supplied with the erection of a parochial house beside the church to accommodate two priests. With the completion of the church and schools the essential structures for the smooth operation of the parish were in place. The many social problems, from unemployment to poverty, that plagued most rural parishes in Ireland remained, and were from time to time exacerbated by denominational hostility. Though McAlister did not experience this hostility in Ballycastle in the raw and violent form in which it manifested

5 PRONI, ED 1/2/63.   6 PRONI, ED 1/3/153.

itself in Belfast and elsewhere, he did encounter antagonism in the local workhouse.

I

Sectarian animosity had long been experienced in the administration of some of the workhouses. Since their foundation in the
1840s, disputes between chaplains and boards of guardians had
occurred especially in those which drew their inmates from
mixed areas. Cornelius Denvir, the bishop of Down and Connor
in a short report to the archbishop of Dublin in 1862 remarked
that the 'Guardians in the Counties of Down & Antrim being
entirely Protestant do just what they please both as regards
chaplains & paupers; But nothing in favour of the Catholic religion which they can avoid doing'.[7] This was too sweeping a
condemnation: not all the guardians were Protestant and some
seem to have worked out reasonably happy arrangements with
the Catholic chaplains for the pastoral care and religious education of the Catholic inmates and their children.

In the Ballycastle workhouse trouble occurred in 1866 when
Jane Millar, a visiting, self-appointed evangelist, began reading
and explaining scripture to all the residents in the wards. Those
confined to bed, who could not leave the wards, were obliged
to avail of Millar's ministrations. And as the sister-in-law of one
of the guardians Millar had more clout than other ambitious
evangelists. McAlister protested to the authorities but they took
no action. He resigned his chaplaincy for which he had been
paid £20 annually.[8] He then took up the case with the Poor Law
commissioners in Dublin, who controlled all the workhouses.
Enclosing the sworn testimony of a Catholic inmate, he pointed
out the violations of the rule about the segregation of the
denominations for religious observances. The master of the

7 Denvir to Cullen, 7 May 1862, DDA.   8 UOb., 6 Sept. 1866.

workhouse claimed that McAlister's witness had threatened Jane Millar with death, and that he had then informed her that, if she objected to the religious activities in the dormitories, he could withdraw to another room. He further charged that McAlister had given orders to his assistant to put both the matron and Millar out.

McAlister rejected this claim. He replied enclosing statements from the assistant, Elizabeth McMullan, denying that he had ever given instructions to throw anyone out, and from the Catholic inmate denying that she had ever issued death threats against Jane Millar. The commissioners, who had refused to hold an inquiry on the grounds that McAlister was no longer attached to the workhouse when he made his complaints, reversed their decision and instructed their inspector to hold an inquiry into the incidents. All those who had been named in the correspondence were questioned.

McAlister objected to the proposal of the guardians to furnish and set aside a room for Millar's meetings and to require an officer of the workhouse to be present, and also to her visiting the sick in the infirm wards, if an officer were present with her. He argued that the rules of the Poor Law commissioners were never intended to be so flexible as to cover such situations. The commissioners duly published their report which found Millar guilty by her own admission of making no distinction between Protestant and Catholic in her efforts to diffuse a knowledge of scripture to all the inmates of the workhouse. Describing her visits as 'intrusive and aggressive' according to the perceptions of the Catholics, the commissioners insisted that visits of a religious nature should be carried out 'strictly in accordance with the rules, and should never be allowed to damage the good order and discipline of the house.'[9]

9 UOb., 30 Nov. 1867.

McAlister's resignation was unusual. Other chaplains who quarrelled with the officials of workhouses remained in office pending the settlement of their conflict. Though he was not generally regarded as contentious, he could be very stubborn and persistent, if involved in disagreements. This determined streak was evident in his dispute with the board of guardians. When the dispute was settled to McAlister's satisfaction, he resumed his duties.

Ballycastle was not scarred by inter-denominational hostility. The relations between the religious communities were happier than in many other similarly sized towns, and the parish priest enjoyed the friendship of many Protestants in the wider district. By 1885 as he entered his sixtieth year the likelihood of his spending the remainder of his life in Ballycastle was strong. He evinced no desire for a transfer elsewhere being anxious to remain where he had built his church, and under normal cir-cumstances his wish would have been realized. The situation changed completely with the death of Bishop Patrick Dorrian on 3 November 1885.

II

Patrick Dorrian had been bishop of the diocese for twenty years, an office he had assumed after spending five years as coadjutor. Before his promotion to the episcopate he had spent thirteen years as parish priest of Loughinisland, following a stint of ten years as curate in Belfast. His career had been spent exclusively in the pastoral ministry and as bishop he had encouraged his clergy to equip their parishes with the pastoral aids of good churches and schools. When he died the diocese was covered with an impressive network of solid, substantial churches, some newly built and others enlarged and refurbished. Many parishes had two or three national schools of which the parish priest was manager, and by 1885 most of these were reasonably well furnished and maintained by the standards of the time then obtaining. Ballycastle was typical of what had happened in Dorrian's episcopate: an older church was replaced and spacious schools were established.

On the day of Dorrian's funeral the parish priests of the diocese met to elect a vicar-capitular who would administer the diocese until a successor was appointed. John McErlain, the parish priest of Ballymoney, who had been Dorrian's vicar-general, would have seemed a likely choice. However, the vote went to McAlister, who was one of the twelve rural deans with a supervisory authority on the bishop's behalf in his own vicariate. The choice of a vicar-capitular by the clergy was often an indication of their views about the succession and so it turned out in this case.

The parish priests of the diocese, after participating in the Mass for the month's mind of the deceased bishop, met in the chapel of St Malachy's College under the presidency of Archbishop McGettigan of Armagh on 26 November 1885 to recommend three names to be submitted to Rome for consideration as candidates for the vacant episcopal office. McAlister topped the poll by a wide margin obtaining twenty-four of the votes cast, and his name went forward as *dignissimus* or most suitable. Second or *dignior* came John McErlain with nine votes, and third or *dignus* was Alexander McMullan, the parish priest of Duneane, with eight votes. Two other priests of the diocese obtained two votes each and one vote went to Michael Logue, the bishop of Raphoe. According to the Roman rescript of 1829 which governed the selection of candidates for episcopal office in Ireland, the bishops of the province were then obliged to submit to Rome their views on the three names which had been chosen, though they were not obliged to recommend any of them. Nor was Rome constricted to a choice from among those names.

The archbishop of Armagh assembled his suffragans on 11

December to complete their part of the procedure.[10] All were present apart from the bishop of Kilmore, who was ill. Their observations on the three priests were brief and factual. They noted that McAlister, aged fifty-nine years, enjoyed good health, had carried out his duties as a parish priest very efficiently, had built a church and parochial house and had given proof of possessing the virtues of piety, prudence and zeal. They therefore considered him suitable for appointment to the vacant see. They also noted that McErlain, aged sixty-one years, had been a very successful pastor, had built a lovely church and excellent schools, and was widely regarded as skilled in business matters. McMullan, who, at fifty-four, was the youngest of the three, had read a distinguished course in Maynooth, was more learned than the other two but by disposition was unsuited to episcopal office. And they added that none of the three had completed their full course of theological study, as the needs of the diocese had obliged them to cut it short.

Had this letter gone to Rome without further elaboration, it would have paved the way for McAlister's appointment. But, though the bishops had fulfilled their obligations, they were clearly uneasy about the qualities of the candidates: they suspected that none of them had the ability, especially in the field of tertiary or even secondary education, to cope with the situation obtaining in Belfast. Accordingly, they wrote a second letter to Cardinal Simeoni, the prefect of the congregation of Propaganda Fide, which had charge of Irish ecclesiastical affairs, raising doubts about their own previous judgement. They pre-

10 One of these suffragans, Woodlock of Ardagh, received a very strong letter of commendation for McAlister from Bishop Brownrigg of Ossory before the meeting. Brownrigg wrote: '... I know pretty intimately the *"Dignissimus"* on the list for Down and Connor and I can safely say he is one of the most apostolic & saintly priests in the Irish Church ... When I was up there about three years ago, I marked him out as the coming man ... I can say he was a model Pastor ... *Moderamen* is, to my humble judgement, what is more especially required in our body at present, and that Fr McAlister has that I'm certain' (Brownrigg to Woodlock, 2 Dec. 1885, ACDA).

sumably thought that McAlister or McErlain would have been regarded as suitable for appointment to smaller rural dioceses but not to Down and Connor.

Justifying their further intervention they pointed out that the good of religion in Down and Connor and indeed in the province of Armagh led them to explain the situation to Rome to draw attention to the particular circumstance of that diocese and especially its principal city, Belfast. They went on to inform the cardinal that Belfast, which held an exalted position among the Presbyterians – who wished to regard it as their Athens – was the seat of one of the principal Queen's Colleges founded to promote the system of mixed education, which had been condemned by Popes Gregory XVI[11] and Pius IX. There were also many other Protestant schools and colleges in that town, which were bitterly hostile to the Catholic church. And though the Catholic religion had made great progress there, many religious activities were still in the early stages of development. Moreover, there was only one parish in the entire town and it numbered 65,000 Catholics – half the Catholic population of the diocese.[12] Consequently, it was essential that the bishop who was appointed should be a man of profound devotion and of exceptional zeal for Catholic education and endowed with outstanding ability and prudence. Whether or not the three clergy who had obtained the votes of their parish priests possessed these qualities they were unwilling to say – the obvious implication was that they did not think so – but they were prepared to submit further information should the cardinal wish them to do so.

The cardinal promptly instructed Archbishop Kirby, the rector of the Irish College and the agent of the bishops in Rome

11 The rescripts forbidding the bishops to take any part in establishing the Colleges were issued in 1847 and 1848 under Pius IX.   12 Though Dorrian was parish priest of the entire town, it was divided into seven quasi-parishes under administrators. From a spiritual point of view that system worked as efficiently as the normal parochial system managed by parish priests.

to let McGettigan know that he should write as soon as possible with the fullest freedom and confidence giving his views and suggestions on the candidate best suited to the bishopric of Down and Connor.[13] Accordingly, Archbishop McGettigan convoked a meeting of his suffragans in Armagh on 7 January 1886. Writing to Bishop Woodlock, who had drawn up their previous statement about the special requirements of Down and Connor, he suggested that their response should be 'more explicit and precise and more to the point'.[14] The bishops of Kilmore and Dromore were too ill to attend but all the others were present. In their letter to Rome they began by repeating the sentiments they had already expressed, especially regarding the excellent pastor, McAlister, and then went on to say that the ecclesiastic to be put in charge of Down and Connor ought to possess exceptional gifts and know how to fight the battles of the Lord courageously and wisely in that most difficult arena. There were three other candidates who had obtained votes from the clergy apart from those already discussed: Two had got two votes each and one, Michael Logue, the bishop of Raphoe, had got one vote. Their investigations had revealed that the other two candidates did not possess the special qualities which the situation required but the third one, Logue, possessed them to an eminent degree. They reminded the cardinal that he and the secretary of Propaganda knew Logue, having met him in Rome in the previous May, when he had played a large part in their deliberations. Though Logue had only received one vote, they were assured on reliable evidence that many more would have voted for him, had they not believed that the Holy See did not normally transfer a bishop from one suffragan see to another. While this was the wisest policy in normal circumstances they thought that such a rule should not apply in the peculiar situation of Down and Connor, especially when the circumstances of

13 McGettigan to Woodlock (copy of letter), 27 Dec. 1885, ACDA.
14 Ibid.

place and time and Logue's outstanding gifts marked him out as the most suitable candidate for the vacant see. And the needs of the diocese of Raphoe being less than those of Down and Connor did not require a bishop of such conspicuous ability. They therefore strongly recommended the transfer of the bishop of Raphoe to Down and Connor.

Michael Logue, who was then aged forty-six years, had been bishop of Raphoe since 1879. Ordained in Maynooth in 1866 he had spent eight years on the staff of the Irish College, Paris, before returning to Glenswilly, Co. Donegal, as a curate and then in 1876 to Maynooth as dean of discipline and lecturer in Celtic Studies. Two years later he succeeded to a chair in theology. He had, like many of the Irish bishops, spent several years teaching in a college and was presumed to be much better equipped to deal with the problems of secondary and tertiary education than clergy whose experience had been limited to pastoral work and who had only been concerned with the conduct of primary schools. Of the five bishops who advocated Logue's transfer, four had taught at secondary or tertiary level, and one of these, Bartholomew Woodlock, as a former rector of the Catholic University in Dublin, was particularly conscious of the episcopal struggle for satisfactory university education for Catholic youth. The bishops obviously felt that none of the candidates from Down and Connor possessed the requisite academic ability, intellectual background or scholastic experience to enable him to cope with the educational needs of the Catholics of Belfast and indeed of the whole province of Ulster. The issues at stake were too large, complex and controversial to entrust to someone who lacked practical knowledge of them.

Logue had been summoned to the meeting but when apprised of its purpose took no part in the proceedings. Had he then taken no further steps to influence the decision of Rome, the likelihood of his appointment to Down and Connor would have been very great. In April 1887 he was appointed coadjutor archbishop of Armagh and a few months later succeeded to the see, where he ultimately became a cardinal, but on this occasion he resisted the wishes of his colleagues to move to another diocese.

On his return to Letterkenny he wasted little time in writing to the cardinal prefect to set out the reasons why he deemed himself unsuited to the episcopate of Down and Connor. Pointing out that he would have acquiesced in the wishes of his fellow-bishops, despite the sorrow it would have caused him, nonetheless, on considering the good of religion rather than his own convenience or inconvenience, he felt that there were sufficient reasons for judging his translation to Down and Connor to be inexpedient. He explained firstly that someone from outside the diocese whose appointment had not been sought by the clergy could not undertake the many difficult tasks expected of a bishop of that diocese in promoting the good of religion nor vindicate the rights of Catholics in education without the prompt and strenuous co-operation of the parish clergy – a co-operation that would scarcely be offered to one who was placed over them against their wishes. Repeating the comment about the size of the parish of Belfast and hence the need for sub-dividing it (reserving part of it for the support of the bishop) he added that many rural parishes where Protestants were numerous and Catholics few were scarcely able to support a parish priest. Consequently, the faithful were greatly restricted in their choice of confessors and many prudent people believed that some of those parishes should be united so that they would be staffed by two priests. These changes would require an intricate knowledge of the districts, of the people involved and of the conditions of the parishes, and this a non-diocesan could only acquire with difficulty and after a long time. Moreover, because of the many great works undertaken by the late bishop, the episcopal office there required great skill in temporal affairs, and this he believed he did not possess nor could easily acquire, since he had spent the greater part of his life in colleges. For these and other reasons he believed that a transfer from a diocese, where the duties did not greatly exceed his ability to another where the burdens were numerous and great, would be a great calamity for himself and would bring no corresponding gain for religion.

He concluded his letter by remarking that all that the bishops had heard about McAlister since their earlier meeting had not only confirmed but also enhanced their high estimation of him. His zeal, prudence and piety had been praised by all. Trustworthy pastors had testified that he had made good the deficiency of his theological course by personal study and was therefore regarded as learned in theology by his colleagues. Because of his suavity and other conciliatory gifts, both priests and people greatly desired to have him as their bishop.[15]

The appointment to Down and Connor was discussed by the cardinals of Propaganda at a plenary congregation on 8 February 1886. They decided to submit McAlister's name to the pope, and six days later the pope accepted their recommendation.

No account of their deliberations survives, and the factors which swayed them in McAlister's favour cannot be definitely known. It seems likely that they would have pressed for Logue's appointment had there been any serious objection to McAlister on the part of the bishops of the Armagh province. But as the bishop of Raphoe had made a convincing case for his own unsuitability and had reinforced the case for McAlister's nomination, there was no overpowering reason to transfer him against his will. Logue's fear that he might not enjoy the co-operation of the priests of Down and Connor may well have weighed with the cardinals. They were always keen to avoid choosing bishops who might provoke or perpetuate divisions or

15 APF, *Acta*, 256, ff 111r–124r.

disputes, and may have calculated that it was better to select McAlister, who had been deemed eligible by bishops and priests for the episcopate, rather than risk the choice of one who, despite greater ability in the field of education, might not receive the acceptance and support which were necessary for a successful and harmonious episcopate.[16]

III

McAlister's episcopal ordination took place in St Patrick's Church, Belfast on 28 March. Archbishop McGettigan was too feeble to officiate, although he presided; his place was taken by Bishop Thomas Nulty of Meath, who was assisted by Bishop Bartholomew Woodlock of Ardagh and by Bishop James Donnelly of Clogher. The special sermon was preached by Bishop Michael Logue. Taking as his text Acts 20:28, which referred to the duties of the bishop's office, he advised McAlister to do as his predecessor so effectively had done and provide a good sound system of education uncontaminated by any tainted source. And as it was a bishop's duty to provide for the wants of God's poor, so, too, he was obliged to promote the civil progress of his people. He then went on to paint a grim picture of the difficulties and opposition awaiting McAlister:

> Though our faith be no longer assailed by open persecution or the no less dangerous weapon of ridicule and calumny, though Catholics can hold up their heads and fearlessly assert their equality, still there are a thousand subtle influences which tend to sap the foundations of their faith. Dangerous literature, dangerous associations, that material spirit which is begotten of an entire devotion to all the affairs of the world, above all a godless

16 Logue was named coadjutor archbishop of Armagh in 1887. On that occasion he obtained 43 of the 51 votes cast. The candidate who came second received only three votes and the other votes were split among five priests. (APF, *Acta*, 257, ff 106r–109v)

28

system of education, do more to rob the soul of the precious gift of faith than undisguised attacks or open persecution.

These are evils with which every Bishop has to contend at the present time but nowhere must they be met with such courage, energy, zeal and sleepless vigilance as in this centre of industry and activity. It is but a few years ago since the struggle of the Church in this ancient diocese of St Malachy was a struggle for bare life. Still she finds herself here as in an enemy's country surrounded by influences which are hostile to the freedom of her action and the success of her mission. Here those enemies which she has elsewhere either outlived or overcome meet her face to face in every effort she makes for the amelioration of the people.

Methods of opposition which have elsewhere yielded to the enlightenment of the age and the spirit of tolerance are here to be encountered in the full freshness of their fanatical vigour. Here we find the very stronghold of that worse than Pagan system of education, which has already made such sad havoc of Christian faith, and to which the enemies of religion look forward with such confidence as the surest means of eradicating from the minds of future generations every vestige of supernatural belief. Truly then, if it be the first duty of a Christian Bishop to guard the purity of the faith among his people, that duty falls with particular force to the lot of the good Bishop upon whose head the episcopal unction is still fresh.

Logue in the excitement of the occasion had allowed his rhetoric to degenerate into hyperbole. Education in Ireland was certainly not pagan. The malign forces which were allegedly operating so successfully in the schools and colleges would have surprised some of Logue's own colleagues. Though they chafed under restrictions about placing religious symbols in primary schools and the times set aside for catechetical instruction, the national system was in effect denominational. Both at secondary and tertiary level some of their demands had been met and acceptable education was available for the small numbers who could afford it.[17]

17 NW, 29 Mar. 1886, MN, 29 Mar. 1886.

Fifty years earlier the installation of a bishop in Belfast would have been marked by the participation of prominent liberal Protestants of the town in the celebrations. But the political tensions which had been building up in that half century had put an end to the inter-denominational harmony and co-operation which made such involvement possible. And the political events unfolding as McAlister entered office reduced even more the opportunities for friendly contact between Protestant and Catholic.

Chapter Two

Home Rule, riots in Belfast, and the Plan of Campaign

POLITICAL EXCITEMENT in the north of Ireland had reached fever pitch by the time McAlister's appointment was announced. The revelation of Gladstone's views on Home Rule in December 1885 galvanized Ulster Protestants to form the Ulster Loyalist Anti-Repeal Committee, and provoked some of the extremists among them to threaten violent resistance to constitutional change in Ireland.[1] Gladstone became prime minister on 1 February 1886, and two weeks later the Catholic bishops, meeting in plenary session, gave expression to the widespread view of their nationally-minded co-religionists, when they declared that Home Rule alone could satisfy '"the wants, the wishes" as well as the legitimate aspirations of the Irish people'.[2] Archbishop Walsh of Dublin promptly conveyed their hopes to Gladstone. But the momentum towards self-government encountered mounting resistance in Ulster.

At a meeting in Hackney, Colonel Edward Saunderson MP, who had become the leader of the Ulster Unionists in the

---

1 The souring of the religious atmosphere explains the attack on Alex Stewart, the parish priest of Ahoghill, at whom shots were fired on Christmas morning 1885. (NW, 4 Jan. 1886)   2 Archbishop Walsh to Gladstone, (FJ, 22 Feb. 1886). Walsh, on behalf of the bishops, also called for a final solution to the land question which, he suggested, could only be brought about by the government purchasing the landlord interest in the soil and re-letting it to the tenants 'at a figure very considerably below the present judicial rents'.

House of Commons[3], announced that, if Home Rule were to be granted, 'the loyal population of the North of Ireland would at once declare civil war'.[4] The prominent conservative, Lord Randolph Churchill, came to Belfast to play the Orange card against Home Rule. In a bellicose speech in London before leaving for Ireland, he denounced Gladstone's policy as one of 'imminent civil war' and predicted that

> before the sun of the British Empire should commence to set, a blow would have to be, and a blow would be struck – the sound of which should go into all lands, and the echoes of which should reverberate into the uttermost corners of the earth.[5]

Cheered through Belfast a week later by 150,000 people, he predicted in suitably apocalyptic tones the fateful loss awaiting Protestants under Home Rule: 'all your liberties, your religion, and all that you value is to be endangered, and the Loyalists are to be sacrificed and the Union dissolved'. He could not have poured oil on inflammable material more dangerously than he did with his battle-cry by telling them that 'honour, religion, liberty' and 'all that makes life worth living', even life itself, was at stake. Lord Arthur Hill, the Grand Master of the Orangemen in Co. Down, foresaw the loyalists of Ireland 'to a man [being] ready to come forward and to maintain those principles in a more practical manner than by words alone'. Though the *Northern Whig*, which represented Liberal Unionist opinion, complained that 'the suppression of facts and the misrepresentation he indulged in can scarcely be regarded by moderate and reasonable Conservatives without some sense of shame',[6] and

---

3 Jackson, *Colonel Edward Saunderson: land and loyalty in Victorian Ireland*, 75–7.   **4** BNL, 10 Feb. 1886. The *Morning News* reported on 6 April 1886 that 100 men had an interview with William Johnston, MP to know the best description of arms they should secure to resist Home Rule.   **5** BNL, 15 Feb. 1886.   **6** NW, 23 Feb. 1886. On 27 Feb. Sedgwick McLean speaking at a Loyalist rally in Bangor declared that 'a civil war, with all its horrors, would be less dreadful than the systematic, never-ending oppression to which they would be subjected were they separated from England' (BNL, 1 Mar.

denounced Churchill for his coarseness and virulence, it was expressing a minority Unionist view.

The Conservative leader, Lord Salisbury, emphasized the concerns of the landlords and the propertied classes when he spoke of defending the integrity of the empire threatened with the separation of Ireland, and of the preservation of the Irish people from the anarchy into which they would fall. Ulster Loyalists, he maintained, were being asked to end the contest that had lasted for generations between England and 'the disaffected portion of the Irish people . . . by a complete and ignominious surrender'.[7] William Johnston MP, the combative Orange leader, announced that he would propose the creation of a provisional committee to guard the interests of Protestants, and ask those Protestants who were willing and able to bear arms to send in their names, and let their opponents know that they meant 'to assemble on the hills and plains of Ulster with their rifles in their hands'.[8] The reorganization and revitalization of the Orange order for political purposes proceeded with increased momentum.[9] Hugh Hanna, a rabble-rousing Presbyterian minister, called on loyalists to enrol in a 'Loyalist Defensive Union' and prove themselves worthy of Derry, Enniskillen and the Boyne.[10]

A special meeting of the General Assembly of the Presbyterian Church was held to consider the 'present serious state of the

1886). Contempt for the alleged fecklessness of Irish Catholics was an ingredient in the anti-Home Rule mix. H.W. Lawlor speaking at Ballymoney said he could object to any parliament 'which would enable lazy Leinster, muddling Munster and conscription Connaught to rule thrifty Ulster' (BNL, 22 Feb. 1886). The Revd H.A. Oliver opined at a meeting of loyalists in Bangor that 'in the South and West they had no honesty nor industry nor sobriety among them and to allow the Protestants of Ulster to be trampled upon by men like these would be ridiculous in the extreme' (BNL, 1 Mar. 1886). **7** BNL, 15 April 1886. **8** BNL, 27 April 1886. He later predicted that Protestants with the bible in one hand and a rifle in the other would fight against being handed over to Fenians, Invincibles and the Dublin Corporation. He claimed that Lord Wolseley and other officers had expressed their determination to surrender their commissions and lead the Protestants in their struggle, if Rome Rule were conceded. (MN, 7 May 1886) **9** Walker, *Ulster politics: the formative years, 1868–86*, 178–92, 240–3. **10** BNL, 8 Feb. 1886.

country', to which the possibility of Home Rule had greatly contributed. With one dissenting voice which gave way to unanimity the clergy and laity numbering one hundred and forty-two deprecated the establishment of a parliament in Ireland, which would inevitably lead to the ascendancy of one class and creed in matters pertaining to religion, education and civil administration. They claimed that no guarantees, material or moral, could be devised which would safeguard the rights and privileges of minorities scattered throughout Ireland, and they maintained that the system of unsectarian national education, which secured equal rights and privileges to all, would probably be replaced by a denominational system in which minorities would be deprived of education except on terms opposed to their conscientious convictions.[11]

One of their members, the Revd R.J. Lynd, dismissed the claims of a numerical majority by arguing that

> they not only estimated who were the people of a land by their numbers but they estimated the people of a land by their character, by their position, by their education, by their wealth, by what they had done for their country, and if they estimated the loyal inhabitants in this way, they had a great balance of all that was truly patriotic and that would really serve the best interests of Ireland, strongly opposed, unitedly opposed to this proposal of Mr Gladstone.[12]

Not surprisingly the atmosphere created by this heady rhetoric led to clashes between Catholics and Protestants. In Belfast minor skirmishes occurred at Carrick Hill, at a time when workers from both communities were experiencing unemployment and hunger, and as many as 1,300 people had to be given free breakfasts on the Shankill Road.[13] As McAlister was

11 BNL, 10 Mar. 1886. 12 BNL, 14 Apr. 1886. Rev. R.R. Kane, the Grand Master of the Belfast Orangemen, advised Protestants never to submit to any government that might be set up in Dublin, never to pay taxes to it and never to recognize it. (BNL, 27 Apr. 1886) 13 NW, 3 Mar. 1886, 10 Mar.

thanking the Belfast branch of the National League for its congratulations on his appointment, he expressed his satisfaction at seeing the Catholics of Belfast 'working in harmony with those of the rest of Ireland in the cause of nationality' and his hope that they would soon obtain the representation on the public boards to which their numbers entitled them.[14] Like his predecessor, Dorrian, he shared the nationalist consensus of the Catholics of his diocese – a consensus that had been honed in the movement for Repeal and, though fractured by the activities of the Fenians, was restored from 1880 by Parnell's campaign for Home Rule.

Gladstone's bill, which was introduced on 9 April, did not propose to transfer any serious, substantive power to the parliament and executive in Dublin. The parliament was to consist of two orders, which though not separate, could at times vote separately. An executive would be responsible to the legislature. All matters relating to the Crown, war, defence, foreign affairs, trade, the post office, customs and excise, were to be reserved to Westminster. Nonetheless, the hostility to the bill, both inside and outside parliament, intensified as the debates took place. In Britain Conservatives and some Liberals attacked it strenuously and arguments about the integrity of the empire and the likelihood of self-government leading to separation jostled with racist contempt for Irish Catholics in an attempt to deny victory to the government. Catholics and nationalists (who were mostly identical) throughout Ireland responded with gratitude to Gladstone's concession. The clergy of Down and Connor, like their colleagues in other dioceses, forwarded to the prime minister resolutions passed at a meeting which acclaimed

1886. By 25 Feb. 42,000 tickets had already been distributed by the Central Food Committee of Belfast, and 2,500 people were being fed every day. **14** MN, 9 Mar. 1886. Patrick Convery, the administrator of St Peter's parish, urged Catholics to sign petitions against a Drainage bill then going through parliament and complained that they had no representative on the Town Council. (NW, 1 Mar. 1886)

Home Rule as the most likely policy to bring peace and prosperity to all Ireland, and especially to Ulster. The Belfast priests declared that they professed the same political principles as the great majority of their fellow-countrymen and desired that in no way would they be 'severed from them in the coming legislation'.[15] Some of those who professed very different political principles were taking non-political steps to thwart Gladstone's plans. An advertisement appeared in the Unionist paper, the *Belfast News-Letter*, requesting 20,000 rifles to arm the opponents of Home Rule.[16]

Only the slightest spark was necessary to turn this tinder into a blaze. And that spark was provided on 3 June when a quarrel broke out at the Alexandra dock during which a Catholic labourer told his Protestant opponent that 'neither he nor any of his sort should get leave to work there or earn a loaf there or any other place'. When this incident became known among the predominantly Protestant workers at the Queen's Island, a hundred or more of them on the following day armed themselves with sticks and bars to attack the Catholic workmen at the dock. The police estimated that 1,000 men followed the assailants. Some Catholic labourers were beaten, others tried to cross the Lagan to safety and James Curran, a young Catholic lad of seventeen, was drowned as he attempted to do so. Seven or nine others were severely injured. The police succeeded in preventing confrontations as the shipyard workers made their way home to the Shankill Road through a hostile Catholic district.[17] On 5 June in similar circumstances a riot was again averted with difficulty.

15 MN, 13 May 1886. **16** BNL, 11 May 1886. The advertisement read 'TENDERS REQUIRED FOR 20,000 SNIDERS IN GOOD ORDER with BAYONETS or SWORDS, to be delivered carriage paid, on or before June 1 in Lots, at certain stations on Northern Counties Railway, as may be required by purchaser – Address, Vigilance Committee, 8335 Office of this Paper'. **17** BNL, 3 June 1886. According to NW 500 of the 3,000 'operatives' at Harland and Wolff's were Catholics.

Curran's funeral took place on Sunday, 6 June and crowds estimated at various sizes between 3,000 and 7,000 accompanied the body from Ballymacarrett to Milltown Cemetery. As it passed by the brickfields, an open space and flashpoint between the Falls and Shankill Roads, a pistol was fired by someone in the funeral procession more 'out of bravado than with any deliberate intention of doing mischief', but it encouraged some of the processionists to rush at the hostile faction which had gathered nearby. The police succeeded in preventing violence as those accompanying the funeral returned home.

On the following evening a Protestant mob attacked a Catholic-owned public house near the Shankill Road, and stoned the police who tried to protect it. Two constables were seriously hurt. On the night of 8 June that public house and another one nearby were again attacked and the police were furiously pelted with stones and bottles, and the town inspector of constabulary was severely injured. News of the defeat of the Home Rule bill on that day intensified the excitement of the rioters. On 9 June police units were again strongly assailed as they made their way into the 'Bowers-hill' barracks on the Shankill Road. They returned fire and killed seven people. On the following day the disturbances spread to other parts of the town – to Great Victoria Street and York Street – and 'two Catholic clergymen were severely maltreated by the mob'. During a visit by Lord Iddesleigh to the convent of the Sisters of Nazareth on the Ormeau Road a hostile mob attempted to attack it, and was accused of hastening the death of the elderly surperioress.[18] Intimidation of workers in mills, factories and public works became rife.[19] The commissioners who inquired into the riots[20] subsequently reported that 'a very determined spirit of hostility [was] shown by the Shankill-road mob to the police'.

18 MN, 7 June 1886.   **19** Ibid., 16 June 1886.   **20** Report of the Belfast riots commission, 3–23; Hirst, *Religion, politics and violence in nineteenth century Belfast*, 174–82.

The looting of Catholic-owned public houses (a trade in which with the butchery business Catholics predominated) and hostility to the police by Protestant rioters became the distinguishing feature of the riots. The police, who were mistakenly thought to be mostly Catholics from the south of Ireland, especially after reinforcements to the number of 400 arrived, were abused as 'Morley's murderers', 'liveried assassins', 'Fenian whores' and 'Southern savages'. In fact there were 598 police under 21 officers in Belfast when the riots broke out. The officers were nearly all Protestant and 330 of the constables were Protestants. They were much criticized at the time for over-reaction but, though the commissioners in their inquiry into the riots were not prepared 'to say that every individual shot was justified', they believed that the resort to fire-arms was justified.[21]

On 17 June 800 of the additional police reserves, who had been transferred to Belfast, left. The general election on 6 July occasioned further troubles. Disturbances were caused in Ballymacarrett by the playing of two bands from rival parties and windows were broken in St Matthew's church and presbytery. Clashes between Catholic and Protestant factions as a band marched to the laying of the foundation stone of an Orange Hall at Ballynafeigh on 13 July led to serious rioting and a head constable, a soldier and two rioters were shot dead. Sporadic violence between opposing groups continued for a few days. By 23 July the town had quietened down, but on 31 July hostilities broke out between bands accompanying the Revd Hugh Hanna's school excursionists and nationalists in a Catholic district.[22] In the ensuing rioting three Catholic-owned public houses were looted and the consumption of alcohol further

21 The *Northern Whig* (10 June 1886) remarked that the Shankill district on that evening was 'in imminent danger of being burned to the ground, and that indeed all the town might have been involved in something like a general conflagration'. The paper explained that the riots were the work of the lowest classes and were often begun by women or mill girls. **22** Report of the Belfast Riots Commissioners, 3–23.

fuelled the violence.[23] The *Northern Whig* placed a lot of blame on 'mobs almost wholly composed of young roughs of both sexes'.[24] The commissioners noted that the riots since 8 June had 'assumed to a great extent, the aspect of a determined attack by the Protestant mobs upon the police and upon the places of business of Catholics residing in the Protestant quarters of the town' They admitted that both religious parties were guilty of 'retaliation and faults' and noted that twenty-eight public houses owned by Catholics were looted and only one or two owned by Protestants suffered the same fate.[25]

On 20 July a memorial adopted at a public meeting of Catholics in Belfast was presented to the lord lieutenant. It listed the factors which led to the riots and which 'should form the scope and subject of inquiring into them'. The remote causes were the inflammatory articles and advertisements in the press, and reckless speeches and sermons; the immediate causes were the premeditated attack on the navvies at Alexandra dock, the wrecking of public houses, the withdrawal of the police from turbulent areas, the want of protection for Catholic workers, the incompetence of the harbour constables, the existence of the Orange society and its conviction that its members would enjoy comparative immunity from local justices, the insufficiency of the police force in Orange districts and public processions with bands and party emblems.[26]

The return of a Catholic school party, some of whom were attacked, led to serious rioting in York Street on 2 August,

23 The commissioners investigating the riots quoted the inflammatory speech made by Edward de Cobain, MP about this incident: 'The unwashed crowd, anxious to get into conflict with any procession that was peaceable and orderly, came right up behind the police, and pelted the citizens with stones, and Her Majesty's police force, instead of turning round upon those who were hurling missiles at a harmless procession, followed the procession with their batons, inflicting the most brutal and ruffianly treatment on the harmless and innocent citizens on their return to their homes' (BNL, 18 Aug. 1886). 24 NW, 2 Aug. 1886. 25 Report of the Belfast riots commission, 3–23. 26 Report of the Belfast riots commission, with evidence and appendices, 629–30.

which despite the presence of 800 police and soldiers, lasted for over two hours and caused another fatality. Disturbances in both the eastern and western parts of the town occurred during the next few days and the police fired on the mob. On 7 August, McAlister ordered the priests to cease hearing confessions in the churches because of the danger of people being attacked as they made their way thither. It was a wise precaution as four deaths occurred in the violence on the Shankill Road, and on the following day an attack on the police who had taken up position in a public house on the nearby Old Lodge Road exploded into a confrontation which claimed a further nine lives. The bishop and his clergy issued an address deprecating the removal of the police and any intention of enrolling special constables. Appeals were made to the congregations in all the Catholic churches on Sunday, 8 August to behave peacefully, to stay within their own homes and not to react violently to any wrongs they might have suffered. McAlister congratulated the parishioners both at St Patrick's and St Peter's churches on their forbearance, claiming that by following the counsel of their clergy they had deprived their opponents of the chance to say that the Catholic community was responsible for the disorders. He advised them that it was their duty to return good for evil, bear with patience the wrongs inflicted on them and refrain from the use of intoxicating liquors.[27]

Some Unionist commentators poured scorn on the bishop's comments, but the *Northern Whig* defended him:

27 MN, 9 Aug. 1886. The commissioners noted that between 8 June and 19 September the principal actors in the rioting were the Protestant mob, and concluded that 'the comparative good conduct of the Catholics must be attributed to the zealous exertions of the Catholic Bishop and clergy who, during the riots, laboured persistently in the cause of peace, and who exercised over their people a great and most beneficial influence' (Report of the Belfast riots commission, 3–23). The *Whig* commented that 'the Protestant mobs ... seem to have taken a savage hatred of the police, a feeling which has unfortunately been encouraged by many people who ought to have known better'. The Catholic mobs showed more restraint because they were not 'so much

We cannot join in the strong language used against the Roman Catholic Bishop of the diocese with respect to his statement that the Catholics have had nothing to do with the riots, and we must indeed admit as we have already admitted, that the Bishop himself and his clergy have done all they could to preserve the peace where they had influence. McAlister cannot, we think, but himself allow that in the Springfield battle and in the firing between the Shankill and Falls Road last Sunday there were two hostile parties, Catholic and Protestant, and for several hours they kept pegging away at each other. To acknowledge this much is simple candour, simple justice.[28]

Trouble continued to flare, stones were thrown at the police and a Catholic worker at the shipyards was assaulted and covered with tar. On 11 August a Catholic mob attacked the tramway depot. In response to a request from the mayor and the executive committee charged with public safety the bishop and clergy successfully called on their people not to hold processions on 15 August (a religious holyday) or to display arches and banners.

And in an interview with the Central News Agency McAlister robustly denied the accusation that Catholics were the aggressors in the riots and gave his view of their origin:

> The riots are due to incitements from the Press, platform, and pulpit of the so-called Loyalist community, and to the attacks upon the Catholic population by Orange parties; and there would have been no riots but for these attacks, which are both deliberate and unprovoked. Let me instance the attack by the Mayor's men, the Queen's Island workmen, upon the dock labourers on the 4th of June, when they murdered one man. That was the cause of these riots. Since then the Orangemen have added to the aggravation. On the occasion of the defeat of Mr Gladstone's Home Rule Bill they followed the advice of their

under the influence of the insane hatred of the police' (NW, 7 Aug. 1886).
28 NW, 17 Aug. 1886. Earlier the paper had praised 'the dignified reserve, worthy of his office' which he had shown since his appointment. (NW, 7 Aug. 1886)

Press, and had a big demonstration to show their joy, which led to a renewal of the riots.[29]

Assaults on the police continued for a further week but after a bad bout on 23 August they could return to their barracks on the Shankill Road, as much of the violence had subsided.[30] On 26 August a deputation which included two magistrates, James Ross and Edward Hughes, who were the largest Catholic employers of labour in Belfast, a barrister, J.B. McHugh, and a priest, John Tohill, travelled to London to put their case to MPs in advance of a debate at Westminster on 2 September. They wanted to have the English law relating to malicious injury extended to Ireland so that a person whose property was looted or pillaged could claim compensation.[31] Thomas Sexton, who had won the parliamentary seat of West Belfast in July, asked why no steps had been taken to find the rifles belonging to the loyalists.[32] In a circular read in all the churches on 22 August McAlister arranged for a collection on the following Sunday 'in aid of the Catholic families who are now in a state of destitution consequent on being thrown out of employment during recent riots'.[33]

On 5 September 'roughs belonging to the Catholic section' threw stones at a Protestant party attending the funeral of an Orangeman. Violence took a different turn on 19 September. A Catholic mob attacked the police in a barrack in a Catholic district to try to force them to release a prisoner who had been

---

29 MN, 13 Aug. 1886. **30** Edward de Cobain, the Independent Conservative MP for East Belfast, accused a police officer of having boasted that he had shot down fifteen Protestants, and suggested that 'the manhood of Belfast' would have to take action to vindicate their character as a community and take effectual steps for the preservation of life and property. (MN, 16 Aug. 1886) **31** MN, 27 Aug. 1886. **32** Ibid., 16 Sept. 1886. The MN suggested that Catholics should form rifle clubs as Protestants had done and thereby obtain ammunition from the government at half cost and avail of the government ranges. (Ibid., 15 Sept. 1886) This would have been a recipe for intensifying the disturbances. **33** MN, 23 Aug. 1886. The collection raised £1,000 (ibid., 30 Aug. 1886).

detained for being drunk and disorderly. In the ensuing assaults on the police three Catholics were shot dead. The commissioners explained that with that incident 'the riots changed their aspect from being mainly an attack by the Protestant mobs on the police to being a similar attack by the Catholic populace'. They commented on the deaths of Catholic rioters:

> this event of 19th September . . . effectually put an end to the insane idea, which had taken deep root in the minds of some of the people, that Her Majesty's Government had selected police from outside Belfast, with the intent and purpose of coercing the Protestant population of Belfast into an acceptance of the Home Rule scheme.[34]

No further serious trouble occurred.

From 4 June to 19 September, thirty-two people died violently and another victim later died from bullet wounds sustained on that day. Of those who lost their lives, two were members of the security forces, five were Catholics and the rest were Protestants, who were mostly killed during assaults on the police. While violence was still occurring the government announced an inquiry into the origins and circumstances of the disturbances, magisterial jurisdiction in Belfast and the constitution and efficiency of the police forces. The commissioners were also requested to investigate the adequacy of the local authorities and police for the maintenance of order and tranquillity in the town and, if necessary, to suggest changes. The court of inquiry, presided over by Sir John Charles Day, a judge of the High Court in England, sat from 4 to 25 October and heard statements from 199 witnesses, including ten clergymen of whom three were Catholic priests. However much the leading clergy and local politicians who were interviewed differed in their political views, they agreed that the possible implementation of Home Rule was the key factor leading to the riots. Senior police officers concurred in that opinion.

34 Report of the Belfast riots commission, 3–23.

Hugh Hanna, the most prominent political activist among the Presbyterian clergy, declared that he shared the view of many prominent people, that civil war would probably break out if Home Rule were achieved. Apart from his evidence the commissioners reported a speech he had made in August in which he had said that the likelihood of that happening induced the police to adopt different tactics in Belfast:

> But when Mr Gladstone surrendered to Parnell and embraced him – when that iniquitous compact and conspiracy was cemented ... it was only natural that the Royal Irish Constabulary, having their own interests largely at heart, should act as they had done . . . The police were the most unfortunate people in the world – if there be no design in their movements – in finding out the criminals who perpetrated outrages against the Protestants and Loyalists of Ireland.

The imported police who came to Belfast, he maintained were one-sided and partisan, were badly mismanaged and had 'savagely batoned' his friends at their Sunday-school outing. He also criticized McAlister for claiming that the origin of the riots lay in the attack of the men from Queen's Island on the Catholic navvies: he on the contrary, 'wanted to take the British public to the origin of these riots in the intolerance of Dr McAlister's own disciples in saying to a Protestant labourer who sought employment among them at the Alexandra Dock that no Protestant would be permitted to earn a loaf of bread'.[35]

Hanna's friend and colleague, William Johnston of Townsend Street Presbyterian Church, also blamed the police for firing at 'Bowers-hill', when the crowds had dispersed, and which caused three deaths. He noted that the people vowed vengeance on the

35 Report of the Belfast riot commission, with evidence and appendices, 373–93. When Hanna accepted the compliment that he represented practically the opinions of all Protestants, the *Northern Whig* dissented from that view, described him as a 'decided Tory' from whose politics many Liberal Protestants differed and who had the support of only about six Presbyterian ministers. (NW, 19 Oct. 1886)

police before the 'foreign policemen' were withdrawn from the Shankill Road.[36]

John Tohill, a priest who taught in St Malachy's College, gave evidence as a secretary of the Catholic committee which had been formed to look after Catholic interests during the riots and so regarded himself as the representative of the Catholic body. He maintained that the remote cause of the disturbances lay in 'the incitements from the loyal Orange and Protestant Press, pulpit, and platform in producing religious hatred of Catholics in our midst'. From the beginning of 1886 a large section of the Protestant community of Belfast was 'almost continually proclaiming that the political course of events were threatening Protestant interests, that Home Rule meant the ascendancy of Catholics, and the extermination of Protestants from Ireland'. Consequently, the worst passions of the Protestant community were aroused against those who were 'ignored in every department of public life in Belfast and who are treated as if they were an inferior and conquered race'.[37] To prove his point he submitted copies of what he considered very inflammatory speeches by Hanna, R.R. Kane (the rector of Christ Church, Belfast and the Grand Master of the Belfast Orangemen)[38] and William Johnston, MP.

---

36 Ibid., 241–9.   **37** In a sermon at St Enoch's Church on 13 June 1886 Hugh Hanna declared: 'the armed servants of that Government are sent to suppress rejoicing loyalty by the sanguinary slaughter of a people resolved to resist a wicked policy and to maintain their full relationship to the British nation and the British crown … At the door of the Government lies the guilt of the bloodshed on that occasion; the guilt of seven innocent lives sacrificed to avenge the resistance of a loyal people to a perfidious and traitorous policy … And so completely did the police frustrate the efforts of moral influence to maintain the peace that it would not be difficult to believe that the people were irritated on purpose to justify the subsequent fire and slaughter that ensued' (BNL, 14 June 1886).   **38** Kane, in an address to loyal Orangemen, wrote: 'I don't believe that those who of late have established a brutal and exasperating regime of batoning and shooting upon the assailed and not the assailants can escape in the end the censure and punishment they merit even as they now receive the strong reprobation and scorn of every humane person in the community' (BNL, 3 Aug. 1886).

Tohill argued that the immediate cause of the strife – an ordinary quarrel between two navvies – was made the pretext for a premeditated attack by the workers of the Queen's Island on the Catholic navvies. He complained strongly about the withdrawal of the police from the Shankill Road and from other 'threatened points' which left Catholic-owned public houses at the mercy of mobs. And he also lamented the failure of most employers, especially Sir Edward Harland, the mayor, to protect their Catholic employees.[39] He alleged that the local press had stirred up hostility to the police, and quoted a remark in the *News-Letter* about men in eminent and influential positions taking care of their friends as an invitation to discriminate against Catholic workers.

Tohill then submitted proposals for the maintenance of peace in the town – several of which were similar to those made by the commissioners: he recommended that two paid magistrates rather then borough magistrates should preside at petty sessions; that a town commissioner of police subject only to the inspector general should have complete control of the police forces in the town; that more police barracks be established in the town; that party processions, the erection of arches across the streets and Sunday-school excursions with bands and flags should be forbidden; that the petty sessions courts be given enlarged powers to deal with rioters; that provision be made to widen the scope for claims for compensation because of malicious injury and that employers be held accountable for malicious injuries received by their employees. His final recommendation was as sweeping as it was impractical: he suggested the suppression of the Orange order, which was 'the cause of all the ill-will, all the disturbance, and all the intoler-

---

39 Harland stated in his evidence that he had 225 Catholic employees before the riots, but that number had been reduced by 50 per cent. McAlister made arrangements with the St Vincent de Paul Society to distribute the funds raised in a special collection throughout the diocese to those who had lost their employment.

ance' to which Catholics were subjected.[40] And he instanced a resolution at the recent celebration which invited Orangemen 'to maintain, if necessary, by force of arms, our independence of the League of Hell of which the traitors who call themselves Nationalists are the leaders'. As an example of this intolerance he also submitted an advertisement from the *Belfast Evening Telegraph* for a pamphlet which, among other accusations, charged Morley, the chief secretary, with granting a license to police officers to shoot Protestants, whether rioting or not.

Tohill also recommended that court cases which involved 'party or religious considerations' in Co. Antrim or Belfast should not be tried by juries. Though he implied that Catholic workers were intimidated into leaving their employment in several firms in Belfast, he also mentioned two by name: Ewart's Mills and the Queen's Island. Referring to a deputation of Catholic workers which discussed with Sir Edward Harland the possibility of their returning to work, he quoted the impression they had received that Harland had no intention of taking them back but wished to keep their names on his books to be able to say that he had Catholic employees. Asked if the Catholics had been blameless from 7 June until the attack on the barracks in Divis Street, he answered 'practically blameless'.[41]

Thomas Peter Carr, a police inspector, vigorously denied that the police, as a mainly Catholic force, acted with cruelty and harshness towards Protestants. Francis Nesbitt Cullen, an assistant inspector, attributed the good conduct of the Catholics generally before 19 September to their clergy and those who helped them. Though he was prepared to commend Hugh Hanna for striving to keep the peace on his school trip, he felt compelled to express his view that Hanna's 'conduct and Dr

---

40 The *Northern Whig* was angered by this suggestion and claimed that Tohill was as extreme on one side as Hugh Hanna was on the other. (NW, 23 Oct. 1886) **41** Report of the Belfast riot commission, with evidence and appendices, 535–48.

Kane's conduct had a great deal to say to the continuance of the riots, as well as the newspaper reports' and blamed them for using 'language calculated to excite passions and arouse angry feelings'.[42]

Not surprisingly, the commissioners traced the origin of the riots to the intense excitement caused by the threat or prospect of Home Rule and found that in the wake of the initial trouble at the docks and the death of James Curran, mistakes had been made in not summoning the borough magistracy and in the subsequent posting and equipping of the police. Tactical errors aggravated the problems of settling or minimizing the confrontation but the root cause was political. The commissioners expressed their view that processions, the erection of arches and bonfires were 'a fruitful cause of rioting and disturbance' and suggested that the person responsible for keeping the Queen's peace should have the power to prevent them, if necessary. They maintained that 'a main cause of the prolonged continuance of the disturbances was the wild and unreasoning hostility exhibited by a large section of the Protestants of Belfast against the police'. Another cause of the continuance was 'the unhappy sympathy with which, at certain stages, the well-to-do classes of Protestants regarded the proceedings of the rioters'. They recommended an increase in the police force with its chief in Belfast having full and complete responsibility for law and order. They rejected the charge that the police had 'acted with cruelty towards Protestants from sectarian motives'. They proposed that two paid magistrates have sole jurisdiction at the petty sessions, and they concluded with the pious and forlorn hope that one beneficial effect of their inquiry would be to render 'all classes of the population of Belfast thoroughly ashamed of the disgrace these disturbances have brought upon their great and prosperous town'.[43]

42 Ibid., 35–77.   43 Report of the Belfast riot commission, 3–23. One of the five commissioners submitted an independent report.

What McAlister, who won praise for his judicious behaviour from the *Northern Whig*,[44] thought of the final report is not known but he was certainly gratified by the cumulative effects of the sworn evidence as the inquiry neared its close. He reported to Rome that

> the sworn evidence has brought confusion to the Tory and Orange party. The Government, magistrates and police officers have given an almost unanimous testimony to the peaceful disposition of the Catholic people and the extreme violence of the Protestants and to the valuable assurance given by the Priests & respectable Catholics in keeping the peace. How much good may result from the inquiry we cannot yet say: but the Orange party have been foiled in their designs. The Catholics have to endure continuous insult from them. To insult them they whistle a tune called "Kick the Pope" & cry "to Hell with the Pope". The Catholics who all love his Holiness have great difficulty in restraining not only their feelings but their hands under such provocation.[45]

The consequences of the riots put a strain on diocesan resources, apart from the human tragedy and suffering which they caused. Lamenting the difficulty of taking up a collection for the new national church of St Patrick in Rome, McAlister remarked in the following January that 'we had to collect all the diocese over & over to keep from starving many hundreds of poor people driven out of work by the deplorable riots of last

44 The *Whig* praised McAlister for entering 'on his duties in a most unobtrusive spirit. From the pulpit he has given no offence to other denominations, and he has not come forward in an extreme political fashion even at a very grave crisis in the history of Ulster and of Ireland. The late Dr Dorrian was not so conciliatory as he might have been. He took delight in keeping apart from Protestants, and even in showing his Nationalist sympathies when they did very little good to the cause he wished to serve. Dr McAlister has, notwithstanding all predictions acted in what we believe to be a more becoming spirit, and we should be glad to see the new Protestant Bishop following his example' (NW, 30 Sept. 1886). The paper was highly critical of the inflammatory part played by the Protestant clergymen, R.R. Kane and Hugh Hanna, in the riots. (6 Oct. 1886)   45 McAlister to Kirby, 24 Oct. 1886, AICR.

Summer & many of whom are still dependent on the charity of their brethren'.[46] He later estimated this number at 2,900.[47] Apart from the serious loss of life and the further deterioration of community relations the disturbances brought suffering to many families whose members were injured or deprived of their jobs and wages. And as always in the case of Belfast riots it was the working class which bore most of the brunt of the violence. The employees and industrialists who lived in the suburbs were protected by distance from the shooting and stone-throwing of the activists who were responsible for the destruction of property, injuries and deaths.

I

As street violence was consuming the energies of many citizens in Belfast, agrarian troubles were occupying the minds of many tenant farmers in other parts of the country. By 1885 a second land war had broken out between landlords and tenants, as a combination of bad harvests, poor crops, competition from meat and foodstuffs from America and Australia and, above all, a downturn in the British economy lowered the prices which Irish tenants could obtain for their stock and crops. In many parts of the country, especially in the South and West, the tenants could not pay their rents, even those which had been judicially reduced in consequence of the land act of 1881.[48] Some landlords began to evict the tenants who could not or would not meet their legal obligations, the most spectacular and highly publicized cases being on the estates of Lord Clanricarde in August 1886. Leading agrarian activists among Parnell's MPs began to advise the tenants to pay only what they could afford. And the association of these parliamentarians with Home Rule meant that their advice was regarded as tainted by Protestant

46 Ibid., 31 Jan. 1887.   **47** Ibid., 28 Apr. 1887.   **48** Donnelly, *The land and the people of nineteenth century Cork*, 313.

tenants in Ulster. Even the Liberal Unionists were not prepared to countenance what they regarded as illegal behaviour by tenants, despite the hardships which the economic crisis inflicted on some Presbyterian tenant farmers.

Though the Catholics of Belfast had no immediate involvement in quarrels about rent, many of them or their parents came from small farms and their sympathies lay with their cousins and relatives in the countryside. Patrick Convery, the vigorous and forthright administrator of St Peter's parish, a farmer's son from South Derry, was the chairman of the Belfast branch of the National League, which since October 1882, had not only acted as an election machine for the Parnellite party but also fought for tenants' rights and land reform.[49] Despite the defeat of the Home Rule bill he continued to encourage his co-religionists to claim their rights to vote arguing that 'the man who neglects to provide himself with this weapon is not a soldier of Ireland'.[50] When Maurice Healy, MP addressed the League in St Mary's Hall, a resolution of sympathy was passed to John Fahy, the curate at Woodford in Galway, who had been sentenced to six month's imprisonment for his part in resisting a landlord on behalf of a tenant. Convery, who declared that 'he would consider it a proud privilege to go into prison fighting for the peoples' rights' went on to advise the tenant farmers 'to hold the little they had, pay their just debts, and clothe their children, and if after that they had anything left they might give it to the landlords, and no person should take a farm from which another had been evicted'.[51]

Three weeks later this kind of advice was given to tenants at national level with the establishment of the Plan of Campaign. Timothy Harrington, the secretary of the National League, in the paper *United Ireland* called on the tenants, who could not

---

49 O'Brien, *Parnell and his party*, 126–33. By July 1886 there were 1,285 branches of the National League, mostly based on parishes, throughout the country. **50** MN, 1 Oct. 1886. **51** Ibid., 2 Oct. 1886.

---

pay the rents demanded by the landlord, to decide on the amount of abatement they needed and, if the landlord refused to accept the reduced rent, to hand it over to a local management committee, which would then lodge it with a trustee. If, as a result, tenants were evicted they would then receive financial assistance from the fund in proportion to their contribution, and when local committees could no longer provide the necessary help, the National League would offer support. The farms from which tenants had been evicted were to be left empty and landlords who carried out evictions were to be boycotted.[52]

The Plan of Campaign struck a sympathetic chord with the nationalists of Down and Connor. But the association of the Plan with nationalist politicians prevented most Protestant tenants from joining with their Catholic colleagues in making use of it in their struggle with landlords. Consequently, large landlords like Lord Londonderry and Lord Downshire could successfully offer their Protestant tenants smaller reductions than were sought, and Catholic tenants on their own were unable to mobilise effectively against the landlords.[53] The hostility of the *Northern Whig*, the mouthpiece of Liberal Unionism, further weakened the appeal of the Plan in North East Ulster. When as a result of the judgement at the trial of John Dillon, MP, one of

---

52 UI, 23 Oct. 1886. **53** MN, 15 Jan. 1887. Lord Londonderry's tenants in North Down sent a deputation to him which included two Presbyterian ministers to seek an abatement of 30 per cent. Despite their encomiastic remarks about his high office as Lord Lieutenant, he listened to them for only forty minutes and read a prepared statement offering them a reduction of 15 per cent. They accepted his meagre offer. Londonderry had an estate of 23,554 acres worth £34,484 per annum. Several Ulster landlords at Randalstown, Ards, Draperstown, Hillsborough and elsewhere, were prepared to offer their Protestant tenants only half what was requested. As the *Morning News* remarked the familiarity of landlords as Orangemen with their tenants turned to one of stern resistance when large abatements were sought. John Dillon later addressed the Newtownards Tenant Farmers' Association and encouraged its members to combine to defend their rights. A resolution was subsequently passed by it which, acknowledging that it was composed almost exclusively of Presbyterian farmers, denounced Dillon's imprisonment as 'a most arbitrary act' (MN, 21 Apr., 5 July 1888).

the leading agrarian activists, the Plan was declared by the government to be 'an unlawful and criminal conspiracy', the *Whig* intensified its opposition and claimed that 'Ulster tenants would be very short-sighted to lend themselves to the designs of Irish Nationalists'.[54]

McAlister's sympathies for the struggle of the tenants was strong and consistent. Unable to attend a dinner in Belfast to honour Thomas Sexton, who had won a parliamentary seat for the town in July 1886, he conveyed his appreciation of the members of the Irish Parliamentary Party – 'a noble band of courageous, self-sacrificing patriots' – to the organizers and singled out for special praise their defence of the small farmers:

> The heroic and successful efforts they have made, and are making, to secure to the farmer a legal right to live in his humble but virtuous home, and thereby to stem the annual tide of emigration which has well-nigh exhausted the life of our country, and led so many of our race to temporal misery and moral degradation in the land of the stranger, have won the heart of Ireland. By teaching our people the power of open and legal combination they have destroyed forever the vile trade of the informer, and earned the blessing of the church.

He looked forward to a happy future when the Irish cause would triumph under the guidance of Gladstone and Parnell, 'one of the most remarkable men of our time'.[55] But in Belfast the possibility of that cause triumphing, however remote, was enough to cause disturbances. A weekend of rioting provoked by political differences occurred in early February 1887.[56] And further strife occurred in August and September occasioned by bands accompanying groups on excursions.

54 NW, 7 Jan. 1887. Bew and Wright, *The agrarian opposition in Ulster politics, 1848–87* in Clarke & Donnelly, *Irish peasants violence & political unrest,* 193–227. Archbishop Knox of Armagh rebuked a member of the Representative Church Body for joining the National League and reminded him that the Church Body should uphold the just rights of property, law and order. (MN, 17 Jan 1888)   **55** NW, 11 Jan. 1887.   **56** Ibid., 31 Jan–3 Feb. 1887.

II

Even before the Plan of Campaign was inaugurated a group of English and Irish Tory Catholic landlords, headed by the duke of Norfolk, Lord Denbigh, Lord Kenmare and Lord Emly, had written to the pope begging him to send a delegate to investigate the situation in Ireland. They complained that the National League, which enjoyed the support of many members of the clergy, interfered in private contracts and imposed its own law by force and intimidation in local areas.[57] The establishment of the Plan of Campaign, and especially the defence of the morality of its policy by Archbishop William J. Walsh of Dublin confirmed their worst fears of clerical unreliability on Irish issues. The archbishop had pointed out in an interview with the *Pall Mall Gazette* that as a result of Gladstone's Land Act of 1881 a dual ownership of the land, that of landlord and tenant, was recognized by law. The Plan allowed the tenants, one of the parties to the contract, to fix the terms on which the contract continued in force – something which the landlords had long done. A tenant who was forcibly ejected from his holding was ejected from the possession of the landlord's property but also from the possession of that which was his own. The landlord was only one of two contracting parties. Rent fixing had therefore to be placed in the hands of some independent authority.[58] As the Plan of Campaign was put into effect on estates in 1886 and in the first half of 1887, Lord Emly forwarded to Rome a letter from John Healy, coadjutor bishop of Clonfert. Healy argued that the Plan contravened all the principles of justice and charity, which he had learned and later taught at Maynooth.[59]

As a result of these and other communications the pope decided to send an envoy to Ireland on a fact-finding mission. The Vatican wanted to have the charges about immoral agrarian

---

57 ASV, Rampolla papers 2A.　58 PMG, 1 Dec. 1886.　59 Healy to Emly, 17 May 1887, APF, SC (Irlanda), 42, ff 715r–717r.

agitation and clerical support for it fully investigated. The papal delegate, Archbishop Persico, was also commissioned to let the bishops know that the pope wished to reserve the problem of tertiary education for Irish Catholics to himself.[60] Persico, an Italian Capuchin, had spent several years as a missionary in India, had been a bishop in Georgia in the United States, and had already been sent on diplomatic missions by the Vatican. A fluent English speaker, who had visited London, when working in India, he had many of the right credentials needed for his assignment. Persico arrived in Ireland on 7 July 1887. He had been ordered to hold consultations with the bishops and to make himself available to those who wished to call with him. Consequently, he spent almost three weeks in Dublin, then travelled to Limerick to meet Lord Emly and thence to Armagh to visit the primate, Archbishop McGettigan.

On 5 August he travelled from Newry to Belfast where he took up residence with the bishop. During the following three days, accompanied by McAlister, he visited all the Catholic churches of Belfast, St Malachy's College, the Christian Brothers' and other national schools and industrial schools and the religious institutions of the Mercy, Dominican, Nazareth, Bon Secours and Good Shepherd sisters. He preached in St Peter's and St Malachy's churches on Sunday, 7 August and on the following day was presented with addresses by the priests of the diocese and by a group of laymen on behalf of the Belfast Catholic Committee. The addresses following conventional forms acknowledged the pope's great love of his Irish children as manifested by his sending to Ireland an envoy of great learning, prudence and experience, and proudly declared that this affection was fully reciprocated. The clergy also pointed out that the Irish people were struggling for the redress of injustice and that their cause was recognized by all impartial observers as

60 Macaulay, *The Holy See, British policy and the Plan of Campaign in Ireland, 1885–93*, 100–33.

just. In reply the delegate praised the loyalty to the pope, which he had encountered, and complimented them on their churches and religious houses.[61] Writing to Cardinal Rampolla, his immediate superior in Rome, he referred to the demonstrations of respect and devotion to the Holy See, which he had experienced, and then went on to remark that Belfast was the bulwark of Orangeism

> where up to a few months ago bloody battles between Protestants and Catholics had taken place. But thanks be to God this time all is tranquil, and the pope's representative walks the populous streets amidst signs of respect and manifest deference. May the Lord be praised! All attribute such a fact to our presence in Ireland, I should say to the pontifical mission. May God grant that it may be so and that things may turn out better.[62]

If Persico thought that he had exercised a calming influence on Protestants or that Protestants were among those on the streets showing him respect and deference, he was wildly mistaken. He had been brought through parts of Belfast inhabited almost exclusively by Catholics, had visited only Catholic institutions and been duly impressed. His presence in those districts of the city mainly occupied by Protestants would have been much more likely to have led to abuse, if not violence.[63]

Towards the end of the year he submitted his report to Rome, which dealt with the major issues he was asked to investigate. Attached to it was a short commentary on the state of the dioceses and on the bishops. He noted that Down and Connor was well equipped with churches, convents, beautiful religious houses and schools, as the previous bishop had done a great lot, indeed almost everything in that respect. Forty years previously,

61 MN, 6–10 Aug. 1887. **62** Persico to Rampolla, 8 Aug. 1887, ASV, Segr. Stato, Ep. Moderna, an. 1888, rubr. 278, fasc. 1, ff 88r-89r and report, fasc. 2, f 133rv. Persico believed that bishops should not publish letters or articles in the press on political issues. **63** The Revd R.R. Kane, the Orange Grand Master, declared on 12 July 1887 that 'before there would be an Irish Parliament there would be civil war' (NW, 13 July 1887).

he explained, Belfast had had only one small church, but at the time of writing it had seven parish churches as well as chapels. The same could be said of the rest of the diocese. In fact, it was the most flourishing diocese in the north of Ireland. McAlister was

> a worthy successor of the last bishop with all the qualities of a good pastor. Scrupulously conscientious, humble, charitable and zealous, he is loved and respected by all. Though a nationalist and supporter of Home Rule, he is moderate and does not publish articles on political matters.[64]

Some precision and accuracy was missing in these comments on the diocese and bishop. Forty years before his visit there were three Catholic churches in Belfast – St Mary's (1784), St Patrick's (1815) and St Malachy's (1844) – but, as he said, the city in 1887 was then well equipped with schools and religious establishments. On political or agrarian issues McAlister's was a much lower profile that that of Archbishops Walsh or Croke, and readers of Dublin-based newspapers would very rarely have seen his name, but he made no secret of his support for the Parnellite party and its agrarian wing, and readers of the Belfast nationalist paper – the *Morning News* – would have regarded him as a firm and convinced supporter of their views.

From Belfast Persico travelled to Derry and thence completed a circuit of the dioceses before returning to Dublin. His report, which was destined to have troublesome repercussions throughout Ireland, was completed and forwarded to Rome four months later.

As Persico continued his round of visits the agrarian problem intensified. As the Plan of Campaign was applied to more estates, Dublin Castle reacted by making greater use of the powers which it acquired through coercion by the Criminal Law Procedure Act of July 1887. As it made its way through the House of Commons both political and ecclesiastical leaders

64 ASV, Segr. Stato, Ep. Moderna, an. 1888, rubr. 278, fasc. 2, 133rv.

vigorously denounced it. The clergy of Down and Connor passed resolutions protesting against 'the inhuman coercive measures of the Government as wholly unwarranted ... as unjust and iniquitous' and claiming that the real object of the bill was to 'force the impoverished tenantry to pay unjust rents, or to purchase their holdings at exorbitant prices, and to silence the voice of Ireland demanding deliverance from the bondage of unjust landlordism'.[65]

Districts were proclaimed and the National League was suppressed in what were deemed to be disturbed parts of the country. One of the most determined activists of the agrarian movement, William O'Brien MP, and his colleague, John Mandeville, were summoned to appear in court at Mitchelstown on 9 September 1887. Though O'Brien did not attend, John Dillon and several British MPs turned up and addressed the gathering. Trouble broke out between the police and sections of the crowd and the police fired, killed two people and injured three others. The 'Mitchelstown massacre' provoked intense anger throughout the country. O'Brien was later tried, convicted and sentenced to prison. Transferred to the jail at Tullamore, he refused to wear prison dress and was left without ordinary clothing. The clergy of North Antrim, meeting in Ballymena, issued a strong protest against the 'barbarous treatment' to which the 'tyrannical Government' was subjecting him.[66] And Patrick Convery, at a meeting of the Belfast branch of the National League, condemned, in the strongest language, the conditions in Tullamore which were slowly killing 'the pure souled patriot, the sterling advocate of the people's rights'. He suggested that sym-

---

65 MN, 14 Apr. 1887. They also protested strongly against 'the malignant aspersions and foul calumnies poured forth on the rest of Ireland by the so-called Loyalists of this northern province, who are urging on the Government in their course of infamous Coercion, and are professing great anxiety about 'law and order', while at the same time their teachings have made Belfast and many parts of Ulster the scenes of violent disorder, lawlessness and crime, undetected and unpunished, and of wanton intolerance towards Roman Catholics in every department of life'.   66 MN, 9 Nov. 1887.

pathy should be shown to the prisoner by giving support to the Plan of Campaign and predicted that there would not be enough prisons to hold the young men who would follow O'Brien's noble example.[67] McAlister may not have made a public statement about O'Brien but the clerical protest would probably not have been made without his support, and he doubtless concurred with the vigorous criticism of government policy made by his colleagues, Archbishops Croke and Walsh.

Catholics in the West Belfast constituency were also concerned about the registration of those among them who were entitled to vote, and the bishop sent a subscription of £5 to the local National League to help that cause. Paying tribute to the advocacy of Catholic claims by Thomas Sexton MP for the constituency, he remarked that it would be 'a great calamity' if the parliamentarians' services were 'to be lost to the popular cause in Belfast'.[68] The Unionist *Belfast News-Letter* took issue with McAlister's comments, arguing that the popular cause 'in the capital of the Imperial Province' embraced Protestantism and Unionism, and reminding Sexton that the popular cause had recently been displayed by the election of the forty members of the town council, not one of whom was a nationalist.[69]

III

Persico duly submitted his findings on Ireland to Rome in December 1887. Though he denounced the Plan of Campaign and boycotting as immoral, he also strongly advised the Vatican not to make any public pronouncements on the Irish question but rather to work with and through the bishops. Pope Leo XIII commissioned Archbishop Walsh, who led the deputation to Rome for his jubilee celebrations in January 1888, to submit a full account of the agrarian issue. It seemed as if the Vatican

67 Ibid., 15 Nov. 1887. 68 Ibid., 29 Nov. 1887. 69 BNL, 30 Dec. 1887.

would weigh up the views of both parties before coming to a conclusion. But the Holy See also came under strong pressure from the duke of Norfolk and his friend Captain John Ross of Bladensburg, who were acting on behalf of the government, to condemn the Plan of Campaign and boycotting, and indeed, to reprobate the participation of clergy in political affairs. Following advice from an expert on moral questions in Rome and without waiting for Walsh's examination of the land question, the cardinals attached to the Holy Office issued a condemnation of the Plan and boycotting in April 1888.[70]

Before the Irish bishops received the official verdict of the Holy Office reports of a papal condemnation of the Plan and boycotting appeared in *The Times*. Then on 27 April, the same day as its sister paper, the *Freeman's Journal*, revealed details of the Roman decision the *Morning News* broke the story to its readers in a short report. Nationalist members at Westminster had concluded that the pope had acted on misleading information. And the fact that he had thought it necessary to state the reasons for his action – reasons which they considered erroneous – was regarded as weakening the probable effect of the document. The actual decree of the Holy Office did not declare on what grounds the condemnation was made, but added that the reasonableness of the verdict could be inferred from the fact that rents fixed by mutual consent could not be broken unilaterally by the tenant, especially as courts were available to adjust rents; that it was unlawful for rent to be extorted from tenants and deposited with unknown persons; that it was unjust that people could be forced not to pay rents with which they were satisfied or not allowed to occupy farms which were vacant. The *Morning News* stated that the Plan of Campaign had been condemned on three distinct grounds, though it did not recount them with complete accuracy. On the following day it struck a

70 Macaulay, *The Holy See, British policy and the Plan of Campaign in Ireland, 1885–93*, 172–311.

combative note when it announced that the people would not be deterred from struggling for their national rights.[71] It poured scorn on the Orange press which was 'in raptures' with the papal decision and was hailing the pope as 'a wise and shrewd man' and 'a valiant champion of religion' only days after cursing his name and lamenting 'the slavish obedience' he demanded from his Irish subjects.[72] A few days later in an examination of the decree the paper pointed out that the decision of the Holy Office would be undoubtedly correct and accepted as such by the Catholics of Ireland, if the assumptions of fact on which it was based were correct. The assumptions were then shown to be groundless.[73]

The reaction of the Belfast nationalist *Morning News* was shared by many nationalist politicians and indeed by bishops and clergy. Archbishop Walsh, the effective leader of the bishops, was in Rome when the decree was issued, and in his absence the other archbishops, Logue and Croke, were uncertain what to do. Eventually they decided to call a meeting of their colleagues for 9 May. Three archbishops and sixteen bishops attended. Both O'Dwyer of Limerick and Healy, the coadjutor bishop of Clonfert, who regarded the Plan of Campaign and boycotting as immoral and unjustifiable were present, and so the contrasting views in the hierarchy were represented. The bishops, in accordance with advice from Archbishop Walsh in Rome, drew up a letter to be sent to the cardinal prefect of the congregation which had charge of Irish ecclesiastical affairs. In it they explained that they were unsure whether the verdict of the Holy Office was to be understood

71 MN, 28 April 1888. The paper explained that the papal pronouncement did not strike at their great national movement nor at the National League, and insisted that the Irish leaders and people would have to carry out their policy in such a way as to save the unfortunate peasantry from unjust evictions. 72 Ibid., 30 Apr. 1888. 73 MN, 2 May 1888. It also quoted an extract published in the *Daily News* from the *Osservatore Romano* according to which the pope only wished that the Irish would defend their rights according to the laws of God.

absolutely or whether it depended on the arguments attached to it, and went on to point out the flaws in its arguments.[74] Nationalist spokesmen and members of parliament continued to attack the decree. The *Morning News*, reporting the invitation to the lord mayor of Dublin to convene a meeting of MPs, remarked that its object would be 'to combat the misleading evidence and unfounded hypotheses on which the Pope, or rather, the Holy Office, has come to such an extraordinary decision'.[75] On 17 May a large public meeting was held in the Phoenix Park, Dublin at which members of parliament boldly rejected any right of the Holy See to interfere in Irish political affairs.[76] The *Morning News* welcomed the politicians' initiative not only as a necessary demand for clarification but also because it wrong-footed the Unionists who claimed that Home Rule was Rome rule.[77]

McAlister was not present at the meeting on 9 May as he was then in Rome, accompanied by three of his priests, to present the pope with a diocesan gift for the golden jubilee of his ordination and to submit the report on the diocese which bishops were obliged to make every five years. The gift was an album of photographs of churches and religious houses in Down and Connor – and, however well-intentioned, it must rate as one of the least valuable gifts which the pope received.[78] Though McAlister therefore played no part in the bishops' meeting there is no doubt that he would have shared the bewilderment and disappointment of the majority of his colleagues at the Vatican's

74 Bishops to Propaganda, 10 May 1888, GDA. McAlister later wrote from Rome to Cardinal Simeoni acknowledging the decree, which had been forwarded to him and stating that he had learned that the bishops had agreed on a way of executing the instructions of the Holy Office. He promised obedience to the Holy See. (McAlister to Propaganda, 13 May 1888, APF, SC 43, f 438r) 75 MN, 7 May 1888. 76 FJ, 18, 21 May 1888. 77 MN, 19 May 1888. 78 The pope subsequently distributed many of the gifts he had been given to dioceses around the world. Archbishop Walsh was unimpressed with some of the vestments that came to Ireland, but McAlister was pleased with 'the beautiful chalice' and set of gold vestments given to Down and Connor. (McAlister to Kirby, 22 April 1889, AICR)

action, and like them would have hoped to limit the damage which it caused. O'Dwyer complicated their position when on 26 May, in response to a plan to hold a meeting in Limerick, he declared that the decree was binding in conscience on all Catholics and that it was a grievous sin to disobey it or to deny the pope's authority to issue it. Bishop Healy publicly supported that claim. The episcopal majority were dealt a much worse blow when Cardinal Rampolla, the Vatican Secretary of State, replied to their letter of 9 May. Rampolla not only told them that the decree obliged all in conscience, irrespective of the reasons attached to it, but informed them of the hurt felt by the pope at the response to the Roman decision and insisted that they summon their people to full obedience to it.[79]

The bishops met in Dublin to discuss the issue further on 30 May and on this occasion McAlister was present. He did not play a prominent part in the proceedings but doubtless lent his support to the majority view, which was articulated by Archbishop Croke and Bishop O'Donnell of Raphoe. They, unlike O'Dwyer of Limerick, did not want to issue a formal statement highly critical of the public agitation provoked by the Roman decree. As a result of their discussions the prelates published four short resolutions declaring that the decree affected the domain of morals alone, that the pope had a right to speak on issues of faith and morals, that he intended to remove things which he judged to be an obstacle to the success of the national movement and they warned their people against the use of hasty or irreverent language about him.[80]

The resolutions were more noteworthy for what they did not say than for what they did say: they gave no guidance on the application of the decree or on the wrongness or sinfulness of continuing to support the Plan of Campaign or boycotting. The majority of the bishops hoped that the agitation would peter

79 Rampolla to Walsh, 25 May 1888, GDA. 80 Minutes of Bishop's meetings, GDA.

out, and that the government would help it do so by legislation which would ease the plight of the tenants. The *Morning News* claiming to concur with other daily papers quoted with approval the English Liberal paper, the *Daily News,* to the effect that the resolutions were an attempt by the bishops to preserve the pope from the hasty and irreverent language of an irritated people. It concluded that the rescript had lost its point, and sympathized with Lord Salisbury at the failure of the negotiations which he had carried out with the Vatican through the duke of Norfolk.[81]

Most of the prelates would probably have feared that such interpretations of their actions could only increase the Vatican's displeasure at their response to its requests. They were extremely keen not to add any fuel to the flames of popular nationalist anger over the decree. A majority of the nationalist MPs had already signed resolutions repudiating the 'allegations of fact' put forward by the Holy Office and insisting that 'Irish Catholics can recognize no right in the Holy See to interfere with the Irish people in their management of their political affairs.[82] Edward Thomas O'Dwyer, the bishop of Limerick, on hearing of a meeting being convened against the decree in his episcopal city, 'authoritatively and officially' informed the mayor that it was binding in conscience and that Catholics who disobeyed it or denied the pope's authority to issue it, were guilty of a grievous sin. He then won the support of the coadjutor bishop of Clonfert, John Healy, for his stand but drew down the stern opposition of the leading parliamentarians, William O'Brien and John Dillon, on his head.[83] McAlister, who was far removed from the scene of this conflict, was not greatly perturbed about it. A couple of weeks later he wrote to Rome

> The excitement over the H. Father's letter has subsided. The enemy made a very vitious [sic] use of it & the Catholic Irish

81 MN, 2 June 1888.   **82** FJ, 18 May 1888.   **83** Ibid., 28 May, 4 June, 12 June 1888.

Patrick McAlister, bishop of Down and Connor, 1886–95

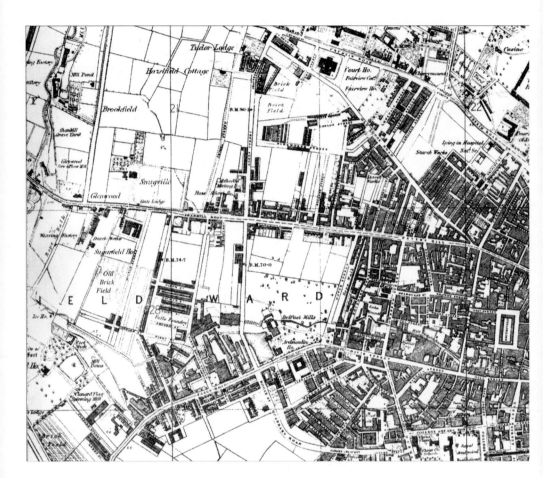

Map of Shankill/Falls, *c.*1865

Cardinal Michael Logue: portrait by Sir John Lavery
Courtesy of the Ulster Museum

The riots in Belfast, as depicted in the *Illustrated London News*,
19 and 21 August 1886: (above) The police charging the mob
in the brickfields; (below) A mob wrecking the tramway
company's depot at Milltown

were stung to the heart at the thought that the Pope, whom they love so much, had, as they imagined, turned against them – The Tory government are making a terrible use of the Coercion Act but it is hoped that they may not be long in office.[84]

It was the Tory press crowing over the discomfiture of Irish nationalists and the harsh application of coercion, rather than the reaction of his co-religionists which concerned him.

A few days later the bishops, at their normal June meeting, called on the government to redress the grievances of the tenants. They sought the establishment of an impartial tribunal to adjudicate between landlord and tenant on rents, and the removal of obstacles which prevented the tenants from having their rights fixed by such tribunals.[85] They doubtless hoped that these resolutions would take some of the heat out of the situation created by the decree but Rome, which was kept informed by their critic, John Ross, about their general slackness in promulgating the decree, was not prepared to let them off the hook. The pope sent a letter on 24 June complaining about the hostile public reaction to his instruction and demanded that the bishops make its terms clearly and plainly known to their people. McAlister did not seem to be much concerned by the attempts of the Vatican to put pressure on the prelates to promulgate the decree. Writing to Archbishop Kirby in Rome he complained about the government sending police and soldiers 'to protect the evicting parties in expelling the poor people from their homes & knocking down their house with battering rams & crowbars.' Expressing sympathy for the poor people suffering these indignities, he remarked that it was 'hard to be quiet in such circumstances'.[86] The Vatican kept up the pressure on the hierarchy to enforce its decree. In November Cardinal Rampolla wrote again to Archbishop Logue of Armagh to

84 McAlister to Kirby, 19 June 1888, AICR.   **85** GDA, 27 June 1888.
86 McAlister to Kirby, 25 July 1888, AICR.

convey the pope's displeasure at the refusal of obedience by Irish Catholics to a decision on moral issues by the supreme teaching authority of the church, and again called on the prelates to exhort their people to obedience.[87] McAlister was one of the few bishops who seems to have bothered to reply.

He pointed out in his letter that the Plan of Campaign and boycotting, which had been condemned by the Holy See, were only practised in his diocese by Protestants against Catholics. In his part of Ireland Protestants and Orangemen, imbued with a great hatred of Catholics, boycotted them extensively. He explained that he had given copies of the papal letter of 24 June to all his priests and asked them to warn their people against making use of methods prohibited by Rome. Since then no attempt had been made to introduce the Plan or boycotting and no public meeting had been held at which they had been approved. He was certain that those practices would not be used in future in his diocese, and he promised to make the cardinal's letter known to his priests so that they could exercise vigilance over their people. The bishop then went on to bewail the sad conditions under which the Catholic people of Ireland were suffering: government ministers had passed laws which empowered the landlords to confiscate the property of the tenants and to evict them from their holdings, and sent soldiers and police to help them carry out those evictions. In a few counties the tenants, driven to despair, committed excesses. The injustices perpetrated by the landlords, of whom many were Catholic, were the cause of the evils and crimes in Ireland. And, if the pope were to condemn the harsh treatment and cruelties of the landlords, that would certainly mollify the angered people and would greatly help the bishops to carry out their sacred duties. He forecast the eviction of some 70,000 people from their homes in the coming winter and the attempted replacement of Catholic by Protestant tenants. Remarking that four million

87 Rampolla to Logue, 10 Nov. 1888, ADA.

people had been driven from their homes and country in the past forty years to cities in England, America and Australia, where their faith and morals were shipwrecked, and not a few of whom, innocent and helpless, suffered from disease, hunger and other evils until they died, he wondered if that very tragic situation lasted another forty years, where the church and Catholic people of Ireland would be. Hence he begged the pontiff to raise his voice lest faithful Catholic Ireland perish.[88]

Just then McAlister had been reminded of the potential danger of Orange hostility. Threats of physical resistance to Home Rule had not ceased with the defeat of the bill in 1886. Colonel Saunderson, the Ulster Unionist leader, declared that the loyalty of his constituents in North Armagh was not merely a form of rhetoric but was supported by the strong right hand of every Irish loyalist. And he went on to explain that Lord Hartington's claim that Ulster would offer every kind of resistance to constitutional change meant that loyalists would use their right hands 'in opposing a dishonourable and traitorous attempt to set over them the most despicable set of miscreants that ever disgraced or defiled the political stage in the world'.[89]

IV

Relations between the Irish church and the Vatican during 1888 had been tense and strained, especially for Archbishops Walsh

88 McAlister to Rampolla, 29 Nov. 1888, ASV, Segr. Stato, Ep. Moderna, an 1893, rubr. 18, fasc. 2, ff 98r-99v. McAlister enclosed an advertisement from a newspaper inserted by Lord Massereene seeking only Protestant tenants for vacant farms in Counties Louth and Meath. At a meeting of the Ulster Land Committee, which acted for the tenants' defence associations of mainly Presbyterian farmers on 10 May 1889 a resolution was passed reprobating the scheme to send Protestant farmers to the South and West of Ireland, and denouncing it 'as a conception of galvanised fanaticism' (McElroy, *The Route Land Crusade*, 75). McAlister later defended the Irish Parliamentary party from accusations made by English propagandists that it had colluded with secret societies to commit crimes. (McAlister to Kirby, 15 Mar. 1889, AICR)
89 MN, 6 Nov. 1888.

and Croke, and some of their colleagues – if not quite so painful for McAlister, whose diocese was not the scene of conflicts between Catholic tenants and landlords. The year 1889 opened on a happier note. Leo XIII, who had celebrated the golden jubilee of his ordination in the previous year, decided to distribute many of the gifts he had received among the dioceses around the world, and in his letter informing the Irish bishops of this plan, referred to his affection for his suffering Irish children and his desire to see that their struggle would not be marked by anything improper. McAlister, like his colleagues throughout the country, was happy to add his comments to the pope's letter, which was read in all churches on 6 January. He enthused about the pontiff's loving words for the Irish people, his sympathy for them in their difficulties, and added his own interpretation of Leo's message which made the pope wish for the success of the rightful cause of Irish self-government. The promise of gifts to the churches of the country was a recognition of their devoted loyalty to the Holy See.[90] Patrick Convery informed the people of St Peter's parish that the papal letter directly contradicted the claims that the pontiff was antagonistic to the desires and aspirations of the Irish people. On the contrary he offered his full support to their downtrodden people.[91]

The respite from bad news afforded by the pope's letter did not last long. Within a month a tragic incident at Gweedore plunged the nationalists of Ireland, and especially of Ulster, into sadness and gloom. On 3 February District Inspector William Martin, at the head of a team of policemen, tried to arrest James McFadden, the parish priest of Gweedore, as he left the church after Mass. McFadden had been an outspoken campaigner for the rights of tenants in the Olphert estate at Falcarragh and Gweedore, and had been sentenced to six months imprisonment in 1888 for

90 MN, 7 Jan. 1889. The pope, in fact, made no comment about self-government, and his good wishes were a benign form of exhortation to Irish Catholics not to ignore his previous counsels. 91 NW, 7 Jan. 1889.

advocating the Plan of Campaign in contravention of the Coercion Act. In the struggle which followed the serving of the writ on McFadden, Martin was killed by some of the parishioners. McFadden and nineteen of those present were duly charged with murder. The *Morning News* arguing that their recent experience of Catholics being excluded from juries could jeopardize the fairness of the trial started a fund to ensure that the accused were given full justice. The four archbishops promptly sent subscriptions of £10 each to the *Morning News* and drew attention to the power of the crown to hold the trial 'where prejudice may run high against the prisoners'. Archbishop Walsh even went as far as to claim that 'under the present system of legal administration in Ireland, it is a matter of practical impossibility to secure a fair trial either for him [McFadden] or for any other prisoner, priest or layman, whom the executive may be really determined to see found guilty on any charge, even on a charge of wilful murder, as in the present case'.[92]

The priests of Down and Connor assembled for a conference in St Malachy's College on 24 April, collected £94, and McAlister, who had contributed £20 of that sum, forwarded it in a public letter to Bishop O'Donnell of Raphoe. Sympathizing with the bishop about the sufferings of his people in Donegal he maintained that

> 'a sentence of Death' as eviction has been aptly termed, often resulting in real death, or followed by a life of misery worse than death, has been put into execution against a large number of your virtuous and faithful people . . . the manner in which the arrest was made was a direct provocation to the people to commit a breach of the peace . . . The subsequent action of the authorities towards Father McFadden and the people exhibits such a gloomy contrast to their action on the occasion of the shooting of the officers, when acting in discharge of their duties, during the late riots in Belfast, that it would require a large fund of credulity not

92 MN, 23 April 1889.

to credit their present zeal with something besides a desire for justice.

He predicted substantial support for the appeal, and his prediction was realized. St Mary's Hall in Belfast was packed to capacity on 8 May to hear speeches by prominent local people in support of a fair trial and of the evicted tenants, and £170 was raised on that occasion.[93] When the appeal closed in 31 October the fund had reached £2,068.[94] The enormous need for that support was highlighted by a report in the *Morning News* in June that 200 families or 1,000 people were in a terrible state of distress in Gweedore.[95] In the event McFadden and twenty-four prisoners were put on trial at Maryborough in Queen's County in October, before a specially selected jury which contained only one Catholic. Sentences ranging from ten years penal servitude to two months were passed on all the prisoners apart from McFadden and one other. The poor and the evicted tenants of Gweedore got much needed help from the McFadden fund.

A further attempt to help evicted tenants generally was made in October 1889 with the founding of the Tenants' Defence Association. Organized at national level and directed by an elected body of fifteen members, its purpose was to defend tenants against combinations of landlords demanding excessive rents or unjust arrears. Tenants were asked to contribute to a fund which would support them, if they were evicted, provided they were willing to submit their cases against their landlords to arbitration. Bishops and clergy who quickly joined and contributed to the new organization hoped that it would escape the censures of the Vatican, which had been applied to the Plan of Campaign, as it called for arbitration in disputes. And, as Archbishop Logue explained, where the principle of arbitration had been applied, it had led 'to peace, harmony and a solid basis of future good relations between landlord and tenant'.[96]

93 Ibid., 9 May 1889.   **94** Ibid., 31 Oct. 1889.   **95** Ibid., 3 June 1889.
96 Ibid., 13 Dec. 1889.

Two months after its formal inauguration in Thurles a convention met in Belfast to establish a branch for Co. Antrim. Five nationalist MPs were joined by some thirty priests and numerous delegates from other counties at a packed meeting in St Mary's Hall. Resolutions were passed committing tenants who wished to become members of the Association to contribute a subscription of three pence in the pound of the rateable value of their holdings. Arrangements were made for the priests and delegates at the convention, who were appointed secretaries and treasurers in their local districts, to hold parochial collections without delay.[97] Speakers advised against accepting any proposal of compulsory purchase by the Tory government on the landlords' terms and pledged support from Ulster for tenants fighting against landlord combinations in Cork and Tipperary. Patrick Convery, encouraging farmers not to relax their efforts in their struggles against landlordism, looked forward to a Liberal victory in a forthcoming election when 'Balfour's tyranny would be swept away and a better, newer, and happier state of things established when they were allowed to make their own laws, on their own soil, and by their own freely-elected representatives'. McAlister sent a letter of support and a subscription of £10. Claiming in it that unjust laws during the past forty years had driven some four million Irish people into exile and inflicted 'unspeakable miseries' on them, he berated the government for pursuing the same policies:

> The present Ministry, not satisfied with the holocausts already sacrificed, pursues with renewed ardour the foolish and wicked work of extermination. If the defensive movement which you have inaugurated contributes in any degree to arrest the progress of this vile work you will deserve the blessings of the Irish nation. I trust your meeting in Belfast on Wednesday may prove a success, and that the farmers of Antrim and Down may see the wisdom of joining their brother tenants in other counties in defence of their common interests..[98]

97 The first list of subscribers from Belfast was published in the MN on 18 Jan. 1890.   98 MN, 19 Dec. 1889.

Though a few Protestant Home Rulers were present[99] and the Catholic nationalists were anxious to make their struggle for tenants' rights broad and non-sectarian, few Presbyterian campaigners for land reform were any more prepared to co-operate with the Tenants' Defence Association than they had been to co-operate with the Plan of Campaign. As the *Northern Whig*, the organ of Liberal Unionism explained, Ulster tenant farmers had a valuable tenant right, which they were not going to jeopardize before the Plan of Campaign.[1]

The Tenants' Defence Association, however, succeeded in holding an important meeting in Ballymoney town hall, which was attended by both Presbyterian and Catholic clergy and laity. The local Presbyterian farmers had long met there under the aegis of the Route Tenants' Defence Association, and though most of them had become Liberal Unionists, when Gladstone was converted to Home Rule, some remained loyal to him trusting that he alone was likely to introduce the necessary land reforms. A Gladstonian loyalist from the Route Tenants' Defence Association, presided, and three nationalist MPs spoke. Resolutions were passed proclaiming distrust in any measure of compulsory purchase introduced by a Tory government, acknowledging indebtedness to the achievements won by the tenants in the west of Ireland and declaring that an equitable settlement of the land question could only be brought about by an Irish parliament directly responsible to the Irish people.[2] The tenants' rights groups, however, in predominantly Presbyterian areas followed the advice of the *Northern Whig*.

99 That small minority was swimming against the powerful tide of the great majority of their co-religionists. At the recent unveiling of the statue to King William at the Orange Hall, Clifton Street, Belfast, Colonel Saunderson, the Ulster Unionist leader, declared that the methods of their opponents were 'murder, treason, intimidation and robbery and the end and aim . . . the disruption of the empire and the subjugation of every Protestant, every freeman to the dominion of Rome and vowed that no alien authority or alien parliament would ever rule over them as long as they had "the hands to strike with"' (BNL., 18 Nov. 1889). **1** NW, 19 Dec. 1889. **2** MN, 3 Jan. 1890.

Nationalist sympathizers in Belfast held a meeting to raise funds for the Tenants' Defence Association and appointed Patrick Convery, the veteran chairman of the local branch of the National League, and Edward Hughes, the proprietor of a large bakery, treasurers.[3] Convery just then wished to retire from the presidency of the National League but was prevailed upon by a gathering of members to continue.[4] A few months later, both the political and agrarian issues that had greatly concerned Catholics throughout Ireland were thrown completely into turmoil by the personal problems of the undisputed nationalist leader, Charles Stewart Parnell. Shortage of funds to sustain the evicted tenants and the bitter split among the members and supporters of the Parnellite party put an end to the Plan of Campaign.

3 Ibid., 10 Jan 1890. **4** Ibid., 11 Feb. 1890. The deep hostility the majority Protestant population of Ulster felt towards the National League was ably articulated by the Orange leader, Richard R. Kane, when he described it as 'an Irish American conspiracy, which they [the Orange party] hated, despised, abhorred, which they looked upon as deriving its inspiration from beneath, and as out-evilling the Evil One in abomination and wickedness' (ibid., 14 July 1890).

Chapter Three

The Parnell Split and the second Home Rule bill

O N 18 NOVEMBER 1890, the *Morning News*, informing its readers that William O'Shea had obtained a decree nisi from his wife on the grounds of her adultery with Parnell, remarked that the verdict of the court would be a 'source of regret to his [Parnell's] friends and to his opponents a source of jubilation'. That understatement was quickly followed by the prediction, that it would not be 'the mad chorus of Parnell's enemies and the enemies of Ireland that would settle the point'.[1] The paper continued to support Parnell when he was re-elected to the chairmanship of the party and rejected Gladstone's 'insolent' letter to John Morley implicitly calling for his resignation.[2] Parnell also spurned Gladstone's plea. Archbishop Walsh denounced him for abusing and betraying the confidence of the Liberal leader, and then on 3 December the standing committee of the bishops expressed its hope that Catholic Ireland 'would not accept as its leader a man thus dishonoured and wholly unworthy of Christian confidence'.[3]

A few days later a majority of the parliamentary party elected Justin McCarthy as its leader. The minority remained loyal to Parnell. The *Morning News*, while bewailing the likelihood of a

1 MN, 18 Nov. 1890.   2 Ibid., 29 Nov. 1890.   3 FJ, 4 Dec. 1890.

fratricidal struggle and hoping that it was not too late for some wise friends to interfere, still refused to say a harsh word against Parnell but admitted that it would be a fatal policy for him 'to force himself on the country and plunge it into a tempestuous excitement'. It therefore suggested that he should give way to avoid bringing about a 'fearful crisis' in his country.[4] If he did not retire he might have to be prepared to find that the vast majority of the Irish people preferred faith and country to the cause of one man.[5] As the days passed its line against Parnell hardened, and as both sides lined up to contest an election at Kilkenny amidst mounting bitterness, the paper blamed him for doing 'irreparable harm' and added sorrowfully that the Orange lodges were delighted with him.[6] His defeat in the election, it declared, should have convinced him that his influence had greatly diminished.[7]

The *Morning News,* which had been owned by E.D. Gray, the proprietor of the *Freeman's Journal,* had been sold after his death in 1888 to a limited liability company in which his son retained one seventh of the shares. The *Freeman's Journal* remained stoutly Parnellite for several months but the *Morning News* became gradually more critical of Parnell and his actions until March 1891, when Edmund Gray, after his return from Australia, insisted that it exchange its partisan for a more neutral spirit.[8] When Parnell in Limerick claimed that the motivation behind the bishops' statement of 3 December was political and not a concern for morality, the *Morning News* accused him of calling the bishops liars, and insisted that they made their statement only when 'the cause of morality and justice was in danger of being trampled on'.[9] And it dismissed his claim that the independence and integrity of the Irish party was being sapped by the British connection as something he thought up only when faced by his own difficulties.[10]

4 MN, 9 Dec. 1890.   5 Ibid., 10 Dec. 1890.   6 Ibid., 19 Dec. 1890.
7 Ibid., 24 Dec. 1890.   8 IN, 20, 22 Aug. 1891.   9 MN, 12 Jan. 1891.
10 Ibid., 13 Jan 1891.

The O'Shea divorce produced a split among the nationalist activists in Belfast, as it did throughout the country. On 4 December a resolution was passed at a meeting of the Belfast branch of the National League 'binding it to a line of strict neutrality in the present crisis' but on 22 December a resolution was introduced rescinding that of 4 December and expressing confidence in the majority of the party which was led by Justin McCarthy. However, the vote on the latter resolution was a tie. In the meantime the president, Patrick Convery, resigned. Recalling that he had spent six years working for the national cause, he explained that he was 'disgusted with the present state of Irish politics' and was not prepared to lose any more of his 'very precious time in political affairs'. The secretary of the branch followed Convery's example for the same reasons.[11] Notwithstanding the vote in Belfast, Archbishop Logue of Armagh believed that priests and people in the north of the country were solidly against Parnell, with the exception of 'a small clique in Belfast and Newry trying to make a noise' which went unheeded.[12]

The Parnellites of the Belfast branch of the National League persisted in defending their champion and obtained a vote of confidence in him at a meeting on 12 January.[13] McAlister wrote to the *Morning News* to remind his people of the bishops' declaration of Parnell's unsuitability as a leader on moral grounds. Though that advice had been generally received with docility throughout the diocese a 'few ardent spirits in the city of Belfast, whose political zeal appears for the moment to obscure their moral perception' rejected it. He regretted that they had 'set their judgement on a question of morality in opposition to the judgement of the legitimate and the highest authority on such questions in the Irish Church'. Since Parnell's

11 Ibid., 23 Dec. 1890.   12 Logue to Kirby, 5 Feb. 1891, AICR.   13 MN, 13 Jan 1891. The resolution expressing confidence in Parnell and hope that the party would be re-united was passed by 57 votes to 34.

leadership had been rejected 'only on account of his public morality' having been 'judicially convicted', those who chose him for their leader would have to take him 'clothed in the convict's dress'.[14]

McAlister's letter drew a lengthy comment from the *Northern Whig*. It praised the bishop for not having any of 'the self-asserting, and dictatorial spirit of his predecessor', who could be 'bitter and unforgiving', and for having so little anxiety to appear before the world that he was scarcely known even by personal appearance. It found this modesty beneficial in a situation where strong sectarian and political differences prevailed, but, on this occasion it argued that, despite his claims that episcopal intervention against Parnell was based solely on moral grounds, he had in fact strayed directly into the realm of politics by warning of the danger of losing the West Belfast seat.[15] McAlister, whose opposition to Parnell intensified as time passed, attended a meeting of Parnell's opponents on 25 January called to arrange a public demonstration of support for Sexton and the majority of the party. He spoke of the calamitous situation that would arise if Ireland tolerated or countenanced the continued leadership of Parnell. And he proclaimed his faith in the loyalty of the Belfast nationalists to 'the principles of social and political morality', and his bewilderment that any section of the Irish people could continue to support Parnell after the revelations of the last few months.[16] The demonstration by the Anti-Parnellites took place in St Mary's Hall on 28 January.

Five MPs and twenty-six priests were among the capacity crowd present. A letter from McAlister was read, in which he expressed his approval of the purpose of the organizers, and his hope that the few Catholics in Belfast who still supported Parnell would realize they were honouring 'a man publicly stained by a crime that should not be so much as named among

14 MN, 20 Jan. 1891.   15 NW, 21 Jan. 1891.   16 MN, 26 Jan. 1891.

Christians' and so see their way to put themselves into harmony with the vast majority of the nationalists and Catholics of Ireland. Joseph O'Connor, the administrator of St Mary's parish, presided and resolutions were passed approving of the part taken by Sexton and McCarthy's section of the party in opposition to Parnell. But a noisy group of Parnellites, who were accused of forging tickets to gain admission, tried at times to disrupt proceedings.[17] They continued to oppose the McCarthyites and formed a Parnellite Leadership Committee, and, though they lost control of the National League, when Joseph O'Connor was elected president,[18] they campaigned vigorously for the 'chief' and published lists of names of supporters in the press.

United Ireland, the Parnellite paper, claimed that the anti-Parnellites had driven Convery, 'the man who has done more than any other for the National cause in Belfast and who was the principal means' of winning West Belfast for Sexton from the chairmanship of the National League. In reality Convery had resigned in protest at the behaviour of Parnell and had made way for Joseph O'Connor, who as administrator of the neighbouring parish of St Mary's, held a very similar position in the Catholic community. The Parnellites, though admitting that O'Connor was 'a genial and kindly and popular priest', regarded him as unsuitable for that post and incapable of leading the Nationalists in their campaigns against powerful Tories.[19]

McAlister threatened to deprive members of the Parnell Leadership Committee of the sacraments in a letter read at all the Masses in the churches of Belfast on 1 March 1891. He complained that the ostensible object of the committee seemed to be

> to honour a man, who by his persistent and impudent attempts
> to force himself on the attention of the country, defiled as he is

17 MN, 29 Jan. 1891. 18 MN, 16 Feb. 1891. 19 UI, 21 Feb. 1891.

with the leprosy of his loathsome crime, continues to outrage the public sense of morality and decency, and tries to subject to his dictation the independence of our country and Church. The Catholic members of the committee, by enrolling their names, have proclaimed their disregard of Christian decency and their contempt for the instructions which the bishops of Ireland considered it their duty to impart to the people ... they have thus become the propagators of public scandal, and have by their own acts placed themselves in the category of those to whom it is unlawful to administer the sacraments of the church.[20]

The *Northern Whig* was appalled by this ecclesiastical punishment and pointed out that Orange magistrates in the past, drinking toasts at grand juries, 'could not have shown themselves more ferocious against those whom they called Papishes than Dr McAlister now does against the Parnellites'.[21] Claiming that the bishop's policy had produced indignation rather than fear, the paper maintained that 'the retiring and kindly prelate' had through his zeal 'committed a great blunder'.[22]

Though the *Morning News* editorialized in favour of this ruthless tactic, hoped for the disbandment of the committee and regretted that Parnell was 'bent on rushing the country into civil conflict',[23] it soon decided to adopt a neutral stance in the struggle between Parnellites and anti-Parnellites. That struggle was further embittered when Henry Harrison, the Parnellite MP, visited Belfast and claiming authority from the central branch of the National League persuaded the secretary of the Belfast branch to let him have the keys of the safe in its office and took away the books and funds of the Belfast branch of the

20 IC, 7 Mar. 1891, MN, 2 Mar 1891. *United Ireland* reported defiantly that an independent branch of the National League was established the next evening. (UI, 7 Mar 1891) At the same time as this ecclesiastical penalty was pronounced against the Parnellites, arrangements were made to take up a collection in all the churches of Belfast on the following Sunday for the relief of distress in the West of Ireland. A little later, money boxes were placed in the churches in support of the pope's plea for the protection of people in Central Africa who were being carried off into slavery. 21 NW, 4 Mar. 1891. 22 Ibid., 6 Mar. 1891. 23 MN, 2 Mar. 1891.

National League.[24] Though the *Morning News* admitted that
the clergy in the north were virtually unanimous against Parnell,
it nevertheless argued that the time had come 'when the spirit
and integrity of Ulstermen should be asserted to crush out dis-
sension ... and to work faithfully and loyally for the common
good of Ireland'.[25] McAlister was angered by the loss of support
from the local Catholic-nationalist organ, and promptly decided
to found one to his own liking. He summoned a meeting in St
Mary's Hall to discuss the launch of a new paper 'to counteract
the evil influence of the *Morning News* in the North, and the
other Parnellite journals, and especially the *Freeman's Journal*
which circulated throughout Ulster'. Parnell was accused not
only of having set an example of immorality but also of having
misrepresented and calumniated his colleagues and of having
tried to exclude religion and morality from politics. Politics,
however, were inseparable from religion and morality and Pope
Leo XIII in a recent encyclical had made it clear that the church,
which had to protect its own rights, also had a duty to advise
and instruct its people. In accordance with the general wish of
the pope to start safe journals for the people, the bishop
explained that they should start a paper to express their views
and protect their rights. Many of the clergy and laity present
promptly subscribed to the new venture.[26] Writing to
Archbishop Kirby in Rome to invite him to obtain the pope's
blessing on his plan, McAlister predicted that, if the new paper
succeeded, it would 'save the cause of religion in Ulster'.[27]
Kirby duly obtained the papal blessing.[28] The *Morning News,*
the *Freeman's Journal* and *United Ireland*, were at the same

24 MN, 3 Mar. 1891. The anti-Parnellites of the National League regrouped
as the Belfast National Committee in sustainment of the Irish Parliamentary
party. **25** Ibid., 23 Mar. 1891. **26** IC, 11 April 1891. Shortly after his
appointment McAlister wrote to Archbishop Kirby expressing his enthusiasm
for publishing any documents or encyclicals from Rome in the Belfast papers.
He thought Protestants were also interested in reading some of those documents. (McAlister to Kirby, 12 Mar. 1886, AICR) **27** McAlister to Kirby,
18 April 1891, AICR. **28** Ibid., 3 June 1891.

time excluded from Catholic news rooms and the news room of
St Mary's Hall.[29]

Throughout the country the bitterness between Parnellites
and anti-Parnellites, fuelled by by-elections grew more intense.
In the by-election in North Kilkenny on 22 December the
Parnellite obtained little more than half the votes of his winning
opponent, the anti-Parnellite. In April in North Sligo, where the
bishop of Killala held aloof and a few priests supported the
Parnellite, who got slightly more than two-fifths of the votes
cast, the resulting defeat was less complete. But the election in
Carlow in July brought another heavy defeat to the Parnellite.

Parnell himself paid a visit to Belfast in May and was given a
rapturous reception in the Ulster Hall by representatives of the
branches of the National League, which had remained loyal to
him, and by ordinary supporters from the northern counties.[30]
United Ireland asked rhetorically if it was true that a deputation
of anti-Parnellites had asked McAlister to condemn the meeting
and to forbid Catholics to attend it, and suggested that the
bishop thought best not to comply with that.[31] The Parnellite
paper, noting that the administrator of the cathedral in Armagh
had told Logue that he might have to refuse the sacraments to
the Parnellites of Armagh, commented sardonically on the fact
that other bishops, apart from Logue and McAlister, did not
refuse the sacraments to political opponents, and wondered
which set of prelates was right or wrong in excommunicating
opponents who had opinions of their own.[32]

In the wake of the visit, relations between prominent
Parnellites and anti-Parnellite clergy in Belfast deteriorated fur-
ther. One man was charged by Joseph O'Connor, the
administrator of St Mary's and president of the National
League, with giving public scandal by receiving Holy
Communion while remaining on the Parnellite Leadership

29 MN, 17 Apr., 1 May 1891.   **30** Ibid., 23 May 1891.   **31** UI, 30 May
1891.   **32** Ibid., 21, 28 Mar. 1891.

Committee, and another claimed that the administrator of St Joseph's parish demanded that he resign from office in the local confraternity lest he also gave scandal to the public.[33] On 26 July a letter from McAlister was read in all the churches of the diocese. Enclosing with it the resolution of all the bishops of Ireland which claimed that Parnell by his misconduct had disqualified himself from the right to lead the people of Ireland, and called on them to repudiate him, he explained that the issue confronting them concerned one of morality and therefore lay within the realm of episcopal responsibility. The solemn judgement of the bishops therefore left 'no room for doubt or cavil on the part of any Catholic who wishes to obey the authority of the pastors of his church'. The *Morning News*, which quoted some of the comments made by priests on the letter, including such denunciations of Parnell as a 'vile and abominable adulterer' lamented the use of this immoderate and abusive language.[34] And *United Ireland* was scathing in its comments on the bishop's intervention. Quoting the text of the Roman decree condemning the Plan of Campaign and boycotting, it argued that McAlister had never obeyed or taught it. On the contrary, despite the solemn authority of the Vatican decree, the Plan of Campaign and boycotting were allowed to flourish from one end of Ireland to the other without a bishop's voice, apart from that of O'Dwyer of Limerick, being raised against them. The paper then went on to refer to 'a species of mental tortuosity known in the diocese of Down and Connor by the name

---

33 Ibid., 6 June 1891. James Rogan, one of the signatories to the address to Parnell, received a letter from James McIlvenny, the administrator of St Joseph's, telling him that if he had put his name to an address having 'for its object the honouring of a public adulterer' he would be asked to resign as promoter of the League of the Sacred Heart. Patrick McKenna, a member of the Parnellite Leadership Committee, was told by Joseph O'Connor that he had committed sacrilege by receiving Holy Communion and was giving scandal by supporting Parnell. He also claimed to have been refused absolution after McAlister's letter had been read. (UI, 13 June 1891)   **34** MN, 27 July 1891.

of "Ballycastle logic"' and explained how McAlister on succeeding to the bishopric from that 'remote parish' had condemned the style of dancing known as the polka but not the waltz. It found the same curious illogic in his declaring 'war against the bucolic and unsophisticated polka' and ignoring the 'voluptuous and often questionable waltz' as in his spending 'his energies in destroying Mr Parnell' who had not been condemned by Rome while leaving the Plan of Campaign which had been condemned uncensored. The bishop was scornfully advised to follow the example of 'the level-headed Archbishop of Cashel and let the people decide for themselves'.[35]

I

The first edition of the new paper, the *Irish News,* rolled off the presses on 15 August 1891 which, as the feast day of the Assumption, McAlister regarded as a propitious birthday. Among its first ten directors were three priests, and clergy also figured prominently amongs its shareholders. And in its first issue it printed a letter of commendation from the bishop alongside one addressed to him from Archbishop Kirby, the rector of the Irish College in Rome. McAlister explained that there was an 'urgent necessity for a daily local journal that will propagate and defend Catholic principles, as well as advocate the rights and represent the views of the Nationalists and Catholics of Ulster' (the two groups which like the great majority of his co-religionists he regarded as conterminous). He drew attention to the warm approval of the project by the pope – in reality a routine conveyance of good wishes and blessings – to which Kirby

---

35 UI, 22 Aug. 1891. McAlister, as he later explained to Rome, had given copies of the pope's letter of 24 June 1888 to all his priests (which ordered them to make the decree known to their people) and asked them to warn their parishioners not to make use of methods condemned by Rome. But he did not publicize the decree with anything like the vigour with which he attacked Parnell.

had referred, and explained that the need for it was highlighted by the overwhelming number of papers conducted by the Protestants of Ulster. He explained that the pontiff welcomed the publication of Catholic journals 'as an antidote against the diffusion of moral poison among Catholic people' and as a means of propagating and defending Catholic principles not only in religion and philosophy but also in politics, science and everything.

Patrick J. Kelly, who had been dismissed from the editorship of the *Morning News*, when that paper changed tack on Parnell in March, was appointed editor of the new paper. Kelly, aggrieved at his dismissal and now given the scope to express his own and his employers' determined opposition to Parnell, did not mince his words in so doing. In his first leader he claimed that their friends in the province of Ulster and three fourths of the people of Ireland had been rudely shocked 'by the introduction of a code of revolutionary doctrines, both political and moral, which they were to accept and support at the bidding of men who had scandalously abused a confidence too generously reposed in them'. Referring to the 'un-Catholic, un-National, intolerant and grossly insulting sentiments' flung at their friends in Ulster, and to the insults and misrepresentations heaped on bishops and priests, the editor promised to try to help his readers form a correct judgement on the great issues facing them. And he promised to 'inculcate respectful attention to the utterances of the "legitimate guides of the people"'. The worst efforts to prop up a bad cause had failed and the nation had emerged victorious from a struggle that was looked upon as a national calamity.[36]

36 IN, 15 Aug. 1891. In a letter to the *Pall Mall Gazette* Gray explained that he had drawn the attention of the managing director of the *Morning News* to the fact that it was being conducted 'in an extremely violent and partisan spirit, and asked him to eliminate vulgarity from its columns in the interests of respectable journalism'. Kelly, by then editor of the *Irish News*, retorted that he considered all Gray's papers beneath contempt. (IN, 20 Aug. 1891)

Not surprisingly *United Ireland* was scathing in its comments on the new journal, disdainfully describing it as 'only a clerical organ and nothing else' which 'would be ruled by priests and their hangers-on'. It took issue with Kirby's dwelling 'so emphatically on the claims of the Catholic church', explaining that such sentiments, while understandable in a purely Catholic paper, were certainly not so when expressed 'so prominently and so aggressively in a journal which we are told has been started to carry to a successful issue Ireland's battle for her political rights'. But it reserved its strongest contempt for McAlister, whom it charged with trying to run Ulster on Ballycastle lines, and wondered sarcastically if the Protestant Nationalist MPs, Pinkerton, Knox and Jordan, were satisfied that 'the old and pious, but, politically very incompetent Bishop of Down and Connor is to be the autocrat of the Ulster Home Rulers'.[37]

In preparation for the launch of his paper McAlister had not only asked Kirby if he could find a Roman correspondent who would send a weekly letter of general interest but had also sought advice and guidance on moral questions from the pope, or presumably through Kirby from the appropriate Roman congregation. He wanted to know if a Catholic could, without sin, teach that Parnell was not unworthy of, or unsuited to, leading a Catholic people in opposition to the wishes of the bishops; if a Catholic could become a member of the Parnell Leadership Committee, a body whose members denied the right of the bishops to pass judgement on Parnell's suitability as leader of the Irish people; and if those who followed Parnell, despite the declarations of the bishops, committed sin?[38] The answer is not known but, as seems likely, if it was influenced by Kirby, it would have been hostile to Parnell.

---

37 UI, 22 Aug. 1891. **38** McAlister to Kirby, 5,7, Aug. 1891, AICR. The *Irish News* soon enjoyed a healthy circulation. At its third annual meeting of shareholders it reported a handsome balance of income over expenditure for the previous year. (IN, 16 June 1894)

The antipathy of the bishop to the *Morning News* was high-lighted by his decision to issue a writ for libel against it in connection with its publication of his circular letter to the clergy, which was read on 26 July. McAlister obviously thought that it had deliberately mangled his words to give a false impression of his meaning, but despite a couple of omissions, the only error it contained would have been recognized, if at all, by readers as typographical, and one which did not alter the sense of his message. The paper reported him as having written 'it is the duty of every priest ... not only to carefully refrain or encourage in any way ... or set the people ... to follow the leadership of Mr Parnell, and also to use every legitimate means to dissuade them from listening to the advice of those who teach disobedience to the pastors'. The passage should have read 'to refrain from encouraging in any way ... the people ... to follow Mr Parnell'.[39] The wider context should have made clear even to the less well-educated readers the central thrust of the episcopal message, and understandably the *Morning News* found the bishop's action 'painful', and, though it did not say so, probably vindictive.[40] And in an exchange of letters with the bishop's solicitors, it was accused of 'skilful and deliberate defamation' but never given the words which were deemed to be defamatory.[41] What had galled McAlister was probably not the mistakes made in reporting his letter but the comments made on it in the editorial of the *Morning News*. While that leader praised the bishop's pastoral 'as a calm and dignified effort to meet a political issue on the score of morality', it bewailed the attacks on Parnell made by the clergy in connection with the letter. It went on to hope for clerical forgiveness 'if we hesitate to believe that good can accrue to either religion or morals by the hurling of

39 MN, 27 July 1891. 40 MN, 7 Sept. 1891. There were a couple of other small errors. The MN reported the bishop as saying that members of oath-bound secret societies fell under the censure of God's commandments, instead of the censure of excommunication. 41 Ibid., 9 Sept. 1891.

charges of adultery and extortion from the Sanctuary at one of our leading public men'. Support for Parnell rather than malicious reporting was most likely the sin that McAlister would not forgive. The *Morning News* duly apologized and in compensation gave £5 to the Mater Infirmorum Hospital.[42] The *Irish News*, however, regretted that the apology had not been made immediately after 'the scandalous attacks' on the bishop but admitted that 'where feelings are dead and reckless persons are blinded by unreasoning passion or disappointment' that was too much to expect.[43]

The *Irish News*, as expected, consistently followed an anti-Parnellite line. It supported the National Federation, the anti-Parnellite association based in Dublin, and reported favourably on its meetings in St Mary's Hall and on the meeting addressed by Tim Healy, an extremely vituperative opponent of Parnell, who denounced his former leader as the most inconsistent man who ever lived.[44] Resolutions of support for Sexton's candidacy for West Belfast were combined with attacks on Parnell for not releasing the funds of the party held in Paris. And James Morris, a curate at Donaghmore, repeated one of the cheapest insults hurled at Parnell when he described him as 'a mere lucrative speculator' from the very beginning.[45] At Parnell's death the paper lamented the inglorious end to a glorious record but insisted that 'his fall was great and humiliating and his moral and political offences so outrageous that he could have no hope of ever seeing that evil record blotted out'.[46] Placards appeared on walls in Belfast announcing 'Parnell murdered! Is it true?; say you priests, is it true?' At a largely attended meeting of the Parnell Leadership Committee there was 'severe denunciation of the conduct of the Roman Catholic Bishop and priests in regard to the National leadership controversy'.[47]

42 IN, 29 Feb. 1892.   **43** Ibid., 1 Mar 1892.   **44** Ibid., 1 Oct. 1891. Phoenix, in *A century of northern life*, 12–17.   **45** Ibid., 18 Aug., 1 Sept. 1891.   **46** Ibid., 8 Oct. 1891.   **47** NW, 8 Oct. 1891.

McAlister writing to Kirby in Rome trusted that the death of 'the wretched man' would bring them peace.[48]

II

The *Irish News* reflecting McAlister's views continued to give its support to Justin McCarthy. Of more immediate concern to it and to the Catholics of Belfast was the fate of Thomas Sexton in the next election. In 1886 he won the West Belfast seat by a mere one hundred votes. It was the only seat within the diocese of Down and Connor (with the exception of a part of South Down) which could be won by a Catholic or nationalist. The great majority of the Belfast nationalists were anti-Parnellites and to help launch Sexton's campaign for re-election they called on Tim Healy's oratorical gifts. Describing Sexton as 'a pearl in the representation of this metropolis', Healy praised the member of West Belfast for obtaining weekly, instead of fort-nightly, pay for the artisans, and for his services to the postal officials, the telegraphists and the local merchants and traders.[49] Sexton had raised issues of concern to Catholics, especially on education, where he conveyed the fears of McAlister about the compulsory attendance of children at schools.[50] He also tried to remedy the Catholics' grievance about the voting arrangements for Belfast Corporation, which, because of the division of the city into five wards, meant that no Catholic could win a seat among the forty aldermen and councillors.[51] McAlister sent a subscription of £10 to the National Federation, the anti-Parnellite association to help its campaign to register voters, and praising Sexton's successful parliamentary career declared that it

48 McAlister to Kirby, 8 Dec. 1891, AICR. 49 IN, 1 Oct. 1891. 50 Ibid., 31 May 1892. 51 Ibid., 2 Mar. 1892. Catholics complained about their under-representation on other public bodies. Of the 21 Harbour commissioners none was a Catholic, of the 15 Water commissioners one was a Catholic and there were no Catholics on the Board of Guardians and among their main appointees in the Belfast workhouse. (IN 29 Jan. 1892)

had raised him 'to an undisputed pre-eminence in the estimation of both friends and opponents in the House of Commons'.[52] Ten priests stood on the platform in St Mary's Hall as Sexton opened his campaign.[53] On the eve of the election the bishop headed the list of Sexton's financial supporters with a gift of £25.[54] But Sexton polled 400 votes less than in 1886 – hard-line Parnellites abstained – and he lost by over 800 votes. McAlister and some of his priests got better value for their contributions to the campaign of Michael McCartan, the anti-Parnellite, who won South Down. Only nine Parnellites were elected, and with Gladstone's Liberal party committed to Home Rule and enjoying the support of seventy-one anti-Parnellites enabled to form a government, the prospects of winning self-government seemed brighter.

Four months before the general election the moderator and several prominent Presbyterian clergy and laity appealed to their co-religionists in England to protect them from the oppression with which they were threatened by Home Rule. They explained that the Roman Catholic hierarchy, which demanded obedience from its people in temporal as well as in spiritual matters, would 'be enabled' to govern Ireland. Protestants would be taxed for Catholic educational institutions, the desecration of the Lord's day would be legalized and Roman Catholicism would be established and endowed. Home Rule would seriously threaten their religious liberties, would nullify many of the benefits of recent imperial legislation and would reproduce 'the condition of lawlessness, outrage, terror and distress, which flourished before the Conservative party took office.[55]

Those prospects had already enraged Ulster Unionists. The *Northern Whig*, whose Liberal form of Unionism had dissolved into a more Tory version, forecast civil war, if Home Rule were to be forced on the loyal parts of Ulster.[56] And in preparation

52 IN, 22 Mar. 1892. 53 Ibid., 28 June 1892. 54 Ibid., 4 July 1892.
55 Ibid., 11 Mar. 1892. 56 NW, 1 Apr. 1892. In an editorial the paper

for the Unionist convention, the Revd William McEndoo, the rector of Tandragee, declared at a local meeting that the English and Scots did not realize the determination of their people to resist Home Rule, and, consequently, it was their duty to let them know that it meant civil war. The object of the great Belfast convention was to declare that they, 'the industrious, the law-abiding, in a word, the backbone of Ulster, who had made Ulster what it was, would wade to the knees in blood before they would submit to Home Rule'.[57] And at the annual meeting of the General Assembly of the Presbyterian Church in June 1892 the resolutions of 1886 forcefully opposing Home Rule and declaring that no moral or material guarantees could be devised which would safeguard the rights and privileges of minorities in Ireland were renewed and passed.[58] The Unionist convention of June 1892 in Belfast attended by the might of the landlord, industrial and commercial power of Ulster and repre-senting all classes met under banners which quoted Lord Salisbury's declaration that parliament had a right to govern Ulster but not to sell it into slavery, and which expressed their willingness to shed blood to maintain the strength and salvation of the empire.[59] Resolutions were passed declaring resistance to the establishment of a parliament certain to be controlled by 'men responsible for the crime and outrage of the Land League,

argued that the conviction that any attempt to force a Home Rule act on the Unionist and loyal parts of Ulster would end in civil war was generally enter-tained. **57** BNL, 20 May 1893. The *Irish News* in a report entitled 'a foretaste of the civil war' gave a short account of an incident at the Queen's Island where two young Catholics were severely beaten and one narrowly escaped being thrown into the dock by a group of rivet catchers. (IN,, 21 May 1892) **58** Ibid., 11 June 1892. A moderator of the Presbyterian church decrying Romish attempts to turn the national into denominational schools claimed that Catholic controlled schools were inferior and that children edu-cated in them were handicapped for life. (MN, 8 July 1890) **59** Walker, G., *A history of the Ulster Unionist Party; Protest, pragmatism and pessimism*, 12–13. Salisbury referring to the fate of James II, who had stepped outside the limits of the spirit of the constitution, had declared: 'if a similar abuse of power on the part of a parliament or a king should ever occur at any future time, he did not believe that the people of Ulster had lost their sturdy love of freedom or their detestation of arbitrary power'. (IN, 19 May 1892)

the dishonesty of the Plan of Campaign and the cruelties of boy-cotting' and predicting 'disorder, violence and bloodshed', if an attempt were made to set up a parliament that would affect their lives, prosperity and civil rights. Thomas Sinclair, the ex-president of the Ulster Liberal Unionist Association, claiming that he and fellow-Liberals had co-operated with their Catholic countrymen in combating civil and religious inequalities and had therefore no desire for a restored Protestant ascendancy, protested against the probable ascendancy of the Catholic church under Home Rule and promised to repudiate the authority of any assembly established in Dublin.[60] The Revd Richard Kane, the Orange leader, declared that his followers would not 'take the crooked stony path of Home Rule, which leads into the wilderness of oppression and plunder' and characterized Gladstone's 'Surrender to Treason Bill' as the 'most vicious and imprincipled scheme of coercion ever devised'.[61]

The Home Rule bill was introduced in January 1893. Though an executive responsible to an Irish parliament was to be established in Dublin, it was not to control matters relating to the crown, defence and foreign affairs and some Irish members would still attend Westminster. Unionist opposition to the bill in Ulster was bitter and intense. It was sternly denounced at meetings and rallies throughout the province. Resistance had hardened further since 1886 and it was again to attract support at every level.

The former chief secretary, Arthur Balfour, who had repro-bated Gladstone's proposed legislation on Home Rule during

---

60 NW, 18 June 1892. On 4 Nov. the NW remarked in a leader that the constitution was 'not flexible enough to hand over some two millions of loyal Irishmen, superior in education, in intelligence, in property, in respect for the laws and devotion to the Crown, to some two millions and a half who have just the opposite characteristics, and who, whatever Mr W. O'Brien and Nationalists such as he may pretend, regard them as foreigners and as enemies'. It also claimed that out of six hundred Presbyterian ministers, twenty were Conservatives, four were Nationalists and the rest were Liberal Unionists.   61 Ibid., 3 Mar. 1893.

the election campaign of 1892 as impractical, contrary to Ireland's economic interests and the wrong response to Irish agrarian needs, came to Belfast in April to support the Unionist cause. Though he had already informed his uncle, Lord Salisbury, the former premier, that he was unsure whether he disliked 'the Orangemen, the Extreme Ritualists, the political disputers, or the R.C.s the most' all of whom he found 'odious' with 'the last' winning out,[62] he established a warm rapport with the Orangemen during his visit. Honoured with the largest demonstration ever seen in Ulster, with marching crowds which took four hours to pass the Linen Hall, he assured his audience that the religious differences in Ireland were deeper and less susceptible to healing than any differences he knew of, which divided people anywhere else in the world. Not only would Ulster's Protestants have to contend with the tyranny of a majority inferior in political knowledge and in political experience, but they would suffer disastrously as their economy would falter under higher taxes and lower wages.[63] What the *Northern Whig* called 'the wealth and intelligence of Ireland' was highly gratified.

The second reading of the bill on 21 April led to violence in Belfast. It broke out on 22 April among the shipyard workers at the Queen's Island, who passed resolutions and put up notices announcing that no Catholics or Protestant Home Rulers would be allowed to work there. Catholics were a small minority of the work force of 9,000, and, when attacked on 24 April, could put up little resistance. Several were badly beaten The police and army were called to the shipyard. As the Protestant workers returned to the Shankill Road they sang 'Rule Britannia' and hurled stones and rivets at three or four Catholic-owned public houses. Estimates of the number of Catholic workmen expelled from the shipyard of Harland and Wolff

62 Quoted in Shannon, *Arthur J. Balfour and Ireland, 1874–1922*, 79.
63 BNL, 5 Apr. 1893, Shannon, Ibid., 64–6.

varied from 500 to 800.[64] Strife also occurred among the girls
working in the mills and factories, and Catholic girls, who
accounted for about a tenth of the workforce in several mills,
were forced to leave work, given their pay and told to stay away
until trouble subsided. The Workman and Clark's yard refused
to discharge Catholic workmen at the behest of loyalists and
Harland and Wolff promptly announced that work would begin
two hours later in the morning. At Barbour and Combe's
foundry, where 800 Protestants and 500 Catholics worked,
there was no disturbance. Richard R. Kane, the Orange leader
whom the *Irish News* accused of firing the ardour of his military
followers, appealed to Loyalists not to interfere with the liberty
of their Catholic neighbours assuring them that '"the hoary
British pharisee" and his infidel accomplice will never persuade
the nation to adopt their disruptive and traitorous policy'.[65] A
Methodist minister appealed to the men at Harland and Wolff's
on 26 April not to damage their political cause in Britain by violence. He had returned from a political mission in Britain where
he had found his Nonconformist brethren ready to oppose
Gladstone's 'insane proposals', and advised them not to jeopardize that support. He promised them that an inquiry into the
conduct of the police would result in justice being done.[66]

Prominent lay members of the Belfast Catholic committee
sought a meeting with the management of the shipyard and on
29 April was assured by Wolff and his manager that everything
would be done to ensure the protection of the Catholic
workers. Several societies of tradesmen at the Queen's Island
also called for all workers to come back. On 1 May most
workmen returned though one Catholic from Barrow-in-
Furness, who had escaped a hanging attempt, would not go
back.[67] The disturbances lasted about a week. Some half dozen

64 *The Times, Daily Telegraph*, 25 April 1893. **65** IN, 25, 26 Apr., 1893.
The *Irish News* recalling Kane's placard 'rise, ye sons of William, rise' claimed
that his boast about never submitting to Home Rule was being realized in the
riots. **66** Ibid., 27 Apr. 1893. **67** Ibid., 1 May 1893.

Catholic-owned public houses were damaged, as were a further twenty houses or shops, a few of which were Protestant-owned and were hit by missiles thrown at the police. About forty-five arrests were made by the police and some of those found guilty were imprisoned for one or two months.

The police, who had been accused of high-handed tactics by Loyalists in 1886, were severely criticized by Catholics in 1893 for adopting a low profile and not interfering in scuffles more promptly and effectively. John Morley, the chief secretary, played down the talk of serious riots when questioned by Sexton in the House of Commons. Referring to a letter from McAlister and the Catholic committee, Morley said that the plans made by the police were made 'by men of the greatest experience and foresight, and with the most absolute impartiality'. But at a largely-attended meeting of the Irish National Federation in St Mary's Hall, Morley's statement was denounced as 'absolutely false and unfounded in every detail' and a demand was made for a full and impartial sworn inquiry into the origin, development and consequences of the riots. Referring to the exclusion of 900 Catholic workers from their employment for a week and the attack on lives and properties in the sight of the police, the meeting also denounced the conduct of those who controlled the police and did not afford protection to Nationalists in times of trouble.[68] The Catholic committee, failing to get any further explanation from Morley, analysed at length his official statement and claimed that on the basis of information supplied to him by his officials and the commissioner of police in Belfast, he had seriously played down the gravity of their accusations. Using as evidence the reports of the local Unionist papers and the statements of G.H. Wolff, the committee insisted that Catholic workmen had been maltreated at, and expelled from, the Queen's Island, that Catholic women had been similarly

68 Ibid., 2 May 1893.

abused at factories, that a Catholic-owned public house had been wrecked and that the police had allowed too much freedom to the mobs hostile to them. No action was taken by the Chief Secretary.[69]

Lord Salisbury who had long believed in firmly resisting the proposed abandonment of his kith and kin and co-religionists in Ulster and, like most Conservatives, was determined to keep the Irish Catholics, whom they despised, tightly enclosed in the Union, visited Belfast in May to support the anti-Home Rule campaign. Rapturously received in the Ulster Hall he resorted to the kind of extreme rhetoric associated with Hanna or Kane:

> That section of Irishmen, of the inhabitants of Ireland, who are led by Archbishop Walsh and Mr Healy – (hisses) – they represent the enemy with which England has contended for centuries (hear, hear) – they represent the enemy against whom England appealed to settlers from Great Britain to come here and help her in her almost impossible task. (Hear, hear) They are the people who have resisted you and threatened you and threatened English interest again and again, in 1641, in 1690, in 1798, and they are the people to whom by a sad and sinister destiny the faint-hearted representatives of this time – to whom these ministers would sell the auxiliaries and the settlers whom they invited and had exposed through many generations in the front of the battle.

Telling his audience what it wanted to hear about the power Walsh and Healy would enjoy in appointing the majority of the politicians in a Dublin parliament, which would select the ministers who would in turn appoint every judge, magistrate and policeman, he predicted that the 'village ruffians of the past' would be the local police of the future.[70] Salisbury's sentiments reflected those of his hosts perfectly.

Minor rioting occurred in August in Newtownards engendered by the excitement over Home Rule. Unusually the blame

69 IN, 26 May 1893. **70** BNL, 26 May 1893. Roberts, *Salisbury Victorian Titan*, 584–9.

was placed on soldiers. About two hundred soldiers of the Royal Irish Rifles were accused of shouting 'God Save Ireland' and 'down with the police'. Four people were arrested but no serious casualties were reported. Some 500 men, women and children of the Volunteers' branch of the Irish National Foresters' Society accompanied by a band were attacked on their return from their excursion to Toomebridge by stones, and iron nuts and bolts, but no one was seriously hurt.[71] And as the St Matthew's band, with a number of friends, returned from an excursion to Downpatrick through Lagan Village, a crowd shouting insults at the pope and Gladstone, threw stones at it and caused some minor injuries.[72]

Though attitudes to Home Rule closely followed religious lines, some Presbyterian Home Rulers braved the anger of their co-religionists to convey their support to Gladstone. A letter signed by the Revd J.B. Armour of Ballymoney and two clerical colleagues, and bearing in all 3,535 signatures was sent to the prime minister promising to co-operate with men of every class and creed to make local self-government in Ireland a success and calling for an immediate revision of judicial rents.[73] But, as their opponents insisted, the signatories represented a tiny minority.

The Home Rule bill passed its third reading on 2 September but a week later was massively defeated in the House of Lords. With the Conservatives in power from 1895 to 1906 Home Rule was no longer a practical possibility and the threat of violence associated with it diminished.

71 IN, 8 Aug. 1893.   **72** Ibid., 9 Aug. 1893.   **73** NW, 15 Aug. 1893, McMinn, J.R.B., *Against the tide: J.B. Armour, Irish Presbyterian minister and Home Ruler* (Belfast, 1985) xxxix–xliv.

Chapter Four

Problems in education

BY 1886, when McAlister became bishop, the national system of education was almost completely denominational. Every parish in the diocese had at least one national school which was managed by the parish priest. Though the managers appointed the teachers and ensured that religion was properly taught in the schools, the bishops and clergy objected to some rules of the commissioners about the exercise of religion, which they regarded as unnecessarily restrictive. These rules forbade the display of religious symbols in the classrooms and limited the teaching of, and references to, religion to a specified time. The bishops complained to the Powis commission in 1870 about the application of these regulations to schools which were not denominationally mixed, but without success. However, despite Protestant opposition the commissioners of national education did overlook some of their own rules from time to time: they allowed crosses to be cut into gable walls in some schools and permitted religious pictures to remain on classroom walls during combined instruction.[1] Despite their complaints most of the bishops appreciated the beneficial effects of the national system both in educational and religious terms, though some of their number tended to emphasize and exaggerate the restrictions on the expression of religious practice and symbolism in the national system.[2]

1 Akenson, *Irish education experiment*, 351. Crosses were regarded by some Protestants as popish symbols.   2 In his Lenten pastoral of 1895 Cardinal Logue pointed out that one of the chief means of promoting faith and virtue

Between 1886 and 1895 the number of schools under clerical management in Down and Connor and the number of Catholic children enrolled in them continued to increase. Of the five schools which were not under Catholic management but had Catholic teachers on their staffs and were visited annually by the diocesan inspector those at Ballyucan and Garron Point had overwhelming Catholic majorities; those at Strangford and Carrickmannon had smaller Catholic majorities; the Catholic children at Hilden represented about forty per cent of the total enrolment. In 1886 the total enrolment of Catholic pupils in schools under Catholic management and in the five mixed schools was 21,266; by 1895 that figure had increased to 24,030.[3]

During those nine years several new schools under clerical management were opened. In Belfast schools were provided for the districts which became the parishes of the Sacred Heart and Holy Rosary. Additional schools were established in St Joseph's, St Matthew's, St Mary's and St Patrick's parishes. Elsewhere schools were set up in Ahoghill, Armoy, Ballyclare, Bangor, Carnlough, Cloughmills, Kilkeel, Kircubbin, Lisburn and Saintfield. In a few places the renovation and restructuring of older buildings let to their classification as male, female or infant schools.

I

Since the establishment of the national system there had been a significant difference between the numbers enrolled in the

was through the Christian education of youth. He then explained that more than sixty years previously 'a system of education was foisted upon this country which makes a solid Christian education a matter of no small difficulty. It is incurably vicious in principle. By excluding every definite idea of religion during the working hours of the school . . . it tends of its very nature to impress the child with the idea that temporal concerns should hold the chief place in his estimation.' (IN, 25 Feb. 1895) **3** Annual reports of religious examination of Catholic schools in Down and Connor for 1886 and 1896 (Belfast, 1887 and 1897).

schools and those who actually attended on most days during the school year. The provision of more schools in more remote parts of parishes, the growing awareness of the value of education and the encouragement given by teachers, whose salaries benefited from the system of payment by results, stimulated more parents to enrol their children in the schools. But the gap between good intentions leading to enrolment and actual attendance remained large. In 1890 the average rate of daily attendance was a mere 59 per cent. In England the problem of poor attendance and consequent ignorance and illiteracy had been tackled in 1880: parents of children between the ages of six and fourteen years were compelled to send them to school for at least seventy-five days each year and failure to do so involved fines or imprisonment.[4]

Pressure to introduce a similar system of compulsion in Ireland, not least from teachers, mounted a decade later. It was a pressure the bishops chose to resist, and McAlister was among the first to challenge the right of the state to introduce compulsion. At the diocesan conferences on 27, 28, and 29 October 1891 resolutions were passed at the bishop's instigation recording the clergy's 'apprehension of the dangers of any such measure'. Beginning with the claim that compulsory meant free education, which in turn involved taxation and hence involvement by school boards in the governance of the schools, the priests claimed that Catholics in Down and Connor would have 'a small and insufficient representation' on them, and in so far as the control of the schools would rest with the boards, it would pass out of the hands of the pastors with consequent dangers for the exclusion of the doctrine and authority of the church. Arguing that compulsion would interfere with parental rights and press heavily through extra taxation on the poor, they claimed that the church already had sufficient resources at her

4 Akenson, *Pre-university education, 1870–1921*, 536 in W.E. Vaughan, *Ireland under the Union*, 11, 1870–1921.

command to secure an adequate attendance of the children. Maintaining that compulsion had not produced elsewhere the expected effects, they predicted that it would be not only useless but also 'detrimental to the interests of education in Ireland'. Copies of the resolutions were ordered to be sent to the chief secretary for Ireland, the leader of the House of Commons, Gladstone, Morley, Sir Charles Russell and members of the Irish parliamentary party, earnestly requesting them to use their influence to prevent the extension to Ireland of compulsory education.[5] When writing to Rome McAlister presented the problem in stark terms. Explaining that they were faced with school boards and secular schools, he characterized that threat as a grave danger to the faith of the children in the diocese where Catholics represented only a quarter of the population.[6]

The *Irish News* representing McAlister's views gave its approval to the resolutions of the priests and suggested that public and private exhortation to children to attend schools, which had been made as comfortable as possible, was the right approach to the problem.[7] Then it went on to take an even stronger view of the case than the clergy. Its comments were inspired by the support given to compulsion at a meeting of the central executive committee of the Irish national teachers. At this meeting the proposal to appoint a sub-committee to draft a statement 'showing the necessity for free and compulsory education' to be sent to bishops, clergy, MPs and others in public positions was passed. The paper responded to the teachers' demands by maintaining that the state had no right to compel parents 'to give a certain amount of secular instruction to their children'. It insisted that the father of the family alone possessed 'the inherent and inalienable right from the natural law of God to decide on the kind and degree of education of his children' and that the state could not override that right. The family,

5 IN, 31 Oct. 1891. 6 McAlister to Kirby, 7 Jan. 1892, AICR. 7 IN, 2 Nov. 1891.

being the first human society, had inalienable rights to the nurture and education of its children. The moral obligation of parents to give their children an education that was both Christian and suited to their circumstances was imposed by God not by the state. Regretting the existence of a principle current in England about the supremacy of the state and the child being its property, the origins of which it traced to the French Revolution (quoting Danton's dictum that children belonged to the Republic before they belonged to their parents), the editorial warned of the danger of encroachment by the state in the management of schools and concluded by professing loyalty to the views of Pope Leo XIII.[8]

The *Irish News* followed up this moral exhortation by appealing to a statement of the entire hierarchy which had been issued in 1873. In it the bishops had declared that the education of their children was a duty imposed on parents by God himself and that children were obliged to devote themselves to such studies as would suit their state in the world and prepare them for eternity. That was 'the sweet power of compulsion, of which the Catholic church possesses the secrets', and the bishops felt bound to 'look with alarm on these growing attempts to substitute physical for moral compulsion in matters of such sacred importance'.[9] As McAlister awaited the introduction of the bill on compulsory education he grew more apocalyptic about the menaces louring over the church. He pleaded with Archbishop Kirby:

> If your Grace can say a word against it that may reach the Holy Father you will deserve the blessings of Irish children unborn. Unless the Holy See forbid it I fear several of the Bishops are prepared to accept it & it will come as a curse to our country ...

8 Ibid., 13 Nov. 1891. In his encyclical *On the chief duties of Christians as citizens* (1890) Leo wrote that, if the laws of the state were manifestly at variance with the divine law, Christians had a positive duty to resist them.   **9** Ibid., 28 Nov. 1891.

Surely if the Holy Father knew the danger that threatens us he would save us from it.[10]

Archbishop Logue was equally pessimistic. He regretted that some bishops seemed to favour it because of the temporal advantages it appeared to offer. He assured Kirby that he was not tempted by such possible benefits:

As for me, I fear, it is only the thin end of the wedge for the purpose of completely secularizing the schools. I believe that on the day on which the Queen signs a compulsory and free Education Act for Ireland the influence of the clergy in the schools is doomed. If the Bishops unanimously opposed it, it would never be passed. I let Propaganda know what I think of the matter; and if they remain passive, they will have only themselves to blame when the crash comes'.[11]

That bill, the Irish Education bill, designed to make education compulsory for children was introduced on 29 February 1892. At their general meeting of 5 April 1892 the bishops explained that they were unable to approve of direct compulsion in Ireland but would 'highly approve of the enactment of any reasonable measure of indirect compulsion'. They also renewed their protest against the refusal of the Department of Education to allow full religious freedom in unmixed schools in accordance with the recommendation of the Powis Report of 1870 and earnestly requested their representatives in parliament to press that point during the discussions on the new bill.[12] In private Archbishop Logue confirmed his disappointment with this general statement. He expressed his fear that the voice of the bishops was losing its old ring and his hope that parliament would be dissolved before the bill was passed.[13]

10 McAlister to Kirby, 14 Feb. 1892, AICR. On the other hand Bishop O'Dwyer of Limerick told Kirby that he favoured compulsion, if guarantees were given against Catholic children being compelled to attend Protestant schools and against any interference with the managerial powers of the priests in the schools. (Ibid., 23 Mar. 1892) 11 Logue to Kirby, 17 Dec. 1891, Ibid. 12 IN, 6 Apr. 1892. 13 Logue to Kirby, 17 Apr. 1892, AICR.

The hierarchy did not spell out in detail its objections at this meeting but three weeks later its standing committee, comprising eight of its members, did so at length and with great force. The bill was shortly due for its second reading, and the standing committee argued that the bishops had a special claim on the government, not only because of the moral and religious interests of their people, but also because it was through their efforts and those of their priests and people that the national system had 'notwithstanding its many short-comings attained its present extension and efficiency'. They went on to maintain that the compulsory clauses were 'unwarranted by the school attendance statistics of Ireland' and protested against them as 'a grave and uncalled-for interference with the constitutional rights of parents'. Furthermore, they were opposed to the natural feelings of the people, would make the schools to a large extent unpopular, would restrict education to the minimum required by the act and would provide further grounds for making 'the administration of the law odious'. Professing their faith in indirect compulsion, they listed measures which could be taken in favour of that policy. These included the prohibition of employment outside their own homes of children under thirteen years of age, and the exclusion of any provision for the 'half-time system' which permitted children to work part time while attending school. They advised the government to commit to industrial schools those children who were habitually absent from schools, such as orphans, deserted children and those whose mothers were vagrants. They also urged the exclusion from monitorships of pupils whose school attendance had not been satisfactory. And they insisted that, as long as schools conducted by religious orders were excluded from the national system, indirect compulsion would still be fraught with many difficulties and complications. To improve attendance rates or 'indirect compulsion' they recommended the establishment of more schools with, if necessary, compulsory acquirement of sites, the improvement of training facilities for untrained teachers, and the provision of infant schools where local national schools were not convenient for small children. They also requested that teachers, who would lose their fees by the bill, would be fully compensated by the amount of the capitation grant.[14]

The chief secretary, William Jackson, piloting the bill through the House of Commons, pointed out that attendance at schools in England and Wales had almost doubled between 1876, when compulsion was introduced, and 1890. By then the average attendance in Ireland had fallen behind that of England by 20 per cent. In England 80 per cent of those enrolled attended school: in Ireland the figure was not quite 60 per cent. The bill proposed to oblige children between the ages of six and fourteen years to attend school for seventy-five days in each half-year ending on 30 June and 31 December. Employment of children under eleven would be illegal, and of those between the ages of eleven and fourteen would also be illegal unless the child had received a certificate of proficiency from a school. Local authorities such as corporations, or in their absence, the local Boards of Guardians were empowered to appoint half the members of the attendance committee and the commissioners of national education were empowered to appoint the other half of the committee which might number six, eight or ten members. The bill would not apply to many rural areas: in fact it was limited to one hundred and eighteen places, comprising municipal boroughs or towns or townships.[15] Jackson quoted Bishop O'Dwyer of Limerick in favour of compulsion and later quoted an extract from a speech by Archbishop Walsh to a teachers' congress in 1890 in which he declared that he would welcome the introduction of an effective measure for securing the regular attendance of children who rarely attended school if, in some cases, they attended at all.[16]

14 Ibid., 29 Apr. 1892. 15 Hansard (4th Series), I, 969–99 (22 Feb. 1892). 16 Ibid., 974, II, 1490 (22 Mar. 1892).

The members of the Irish Parliamentary Party who took part in the debates did not raise much objection to the concept of compulsion: they concentrated on details which they thought should be altered. Alexander Blaine, MP for South Armagh, maintained that they could not have too much compulsion. Claiming that eight convict prisons in England had been swept away as a result of the education act of 1870, he looked forward to the same beneficial effects attending the extension of education in Ireland.[17] Michael Conway, MP for North Leitrim, while not opposing compulsion, declared that they needed more and better schools.[18] T.M. Healy supported compulsion in the abstract but demanded the same municipal franchise as England enjoyed to carry it into effect, and also asked that the children as in Wales and Scotland should be taught in their own language.[19] Edmond Knox, MP for Cavan, who was a Protestant, drew attention to the under-representation of Catholics on public bodies in Belfast, and hence the danger of their being excluded from the attendance committee. He explained that there was no Catholic among the members of the Town Council, the Poor Law Guardians or the Harbour Commissioners. There was, however, one Catholic member of the Water Commission. He questioned the proposal to give such power to a body that had shown itself exclusive, if not intolerant.[20] John O'Connor, MP for South Kerry, denied the necessity for applying the principle of compulsion as Irish parents were keen to ensure that their children were better educated than they themselves.[21]

Thomas Sexton, MP for West Belfast, like several of his colleagues, drew attention to the plight of the Christian Brothers' schools. Noting that they were not entitled to state aid because of their refusal to exclude religious symbols from their schools – though they were in receipt of such aid in Gibraltar, Calcutta

---

17 Ibid., v, 263–6 (30 May 1892).   18 Ibid., 269–71.   19 Ibid., 271–7.
20 Ibid., I, 993 (22 Feb. 1892).   21 Ibid., 989. Blaine, O'Connor and Conway were all Panellites. Blaine was anti-clerical.

and Newfoundland – he stated that they had schools in sixty of the principal towns of Ireland. In thirty of those towns there was no other school under Catholic management, and so, if parents were summoned for non-attendance of their children at school, they could argue that parliament had made education free but they were being penalized for non-attendance at a fee-paying school. Sexton invited the government to give very careful attention to the bishops' views, and maintained that they believed the biggest need was for more and better schools, more training opportunities for teachers and compulsory power to obtain sites. Favouring indirect compulsion the bishops thought that employment of children should be restricted, that monitorships and other prizes in schools should depend on regular attendance and that industrial schools should be provided for orphans and deserted children. By taking account of the pupils attending the Christian Brothers' schools and those of the Church Education Society the figure for non-attendance was seen to be less than one per cent. Unless the Christian Brothers' schools were brought into the national system, it would be deadlocked in the principal cities and towns of Ireland. Sexton also drew attention to the undemocratic methods of selecting the bodies which would appoint the attendance committees citing the case of Limerick where 400 people out of a population of 40,000 would choose the members. The implication was that Catholics would have no representative on the attendance committee in Belfast, and could not be assured of fair treatment.

Sexton also referred to the mention in the bill of the absence of an efficient school within two miles of the child's home as a reasonable excuse for non-attendance, but pointed out the anomaly that occurred in the case of a Christian Brothers' school which was within that distance and was efficient: the parent was obliged to send the child to that school even though it was not supported by the national system.[22] Other nationalist

22 Ibid., II, 1463–72 (22 Mar. 1892), V, 225–39 (30 May 1892), 1163–66

members also drew attention to the position of the Christian Brothers, claiming that in England their schools would receive grants, but in Ireland were grant-aided only for their classes in science and art. Though Jackson, emphasizing the importance of offering parents the advantages of free education, took note of the fees they would have to pay at Christian Brothers' schools and indicated that he would have to find a plan to include those schools in his legislation, did not do so. And the Liberal Unionist, T.W. Russell, and the Unionist, James Rentoul, representing Presbyterian views, opposed any bending of the rules of the national system to accommodate the Brothers' insistence on having a Catholic atmosphere in their schools.[23] William Jackson, the Chief Secretary, stated that their plan was to free the schools from the payment of 'school pence' and to offer to parents the advantages of free education. He admitted that there were towns where there were no schools other than those conducted by the Christian Brothers and he promised to find some solution to that problem.[24] He also emphasized that education in the national schools would be free. In the context of payment of fees, Sexton highlighted a practice which had obtained in Belfast: an important firm deducted the school fees from the wages of children who attended a Catholic school but did not do so in the case of children, Catholic or Protestant, who attended a Protestant school. It also paid the Protestant teacher £30 per year but paid nothing to the Catholic teacher. The bill passed into law in June 1892 to take effect from 1 January 1894.

(15 June 1892). **23** Ibid., I, 990–2, (22 Feb. 1892), II, 1493, (22 Mar. 1892), V, 1169–70, (15 June 1892). The bishops contacted the Congregation of Propaganda in Rome about the Christian Brothers' schools. They wanted to know whether the Brothers, while maintaining the confessional character of their schools, could submit to the rules of the national board, and thereby obtain grants from it. If so, the Brothers could be patrons or managers or the bishops themselves could be patrons and nominate priests as managers. Propaganda refused permission. (APF, *Acta*, 263, f 83r, 4 Dec. 1893)
24 Ibid., V, 1177–8 (15 June 1892).

Shortly before leaving office Jackson, concerned about the difficulty posed by the Christian Brothers' schools, invited the commissioners of national education in August 1892 to include a conscience clause in their regulations, whereby children could attend a school run by the Brothers without being obliged to be present at religious instruction. John Morley, who succeeded him in that office, pursued this line of negotiations with the commissioners. Protestant members of the commission raised objections and suggested alterations which would have sub-jected denominational schools to school inspections, and their books and regulations to the commissioners' approval. Morley, realizing the problems those recommendations would raise, called for further consultation, and a committee of commis-sioners put forward new proposals whereby denominational schools of three years standing, if they had an average daily attendance of thirty-five pupils and observed the conscience clause, would not be subject to the religious rules of the national board. But this and other suggestions did not provide for the Christian Brothers to use religious emblems and their own books. Further negotiations between Morley and the com-missioners led to the recommendation that denominational schools should be grant-aided but on condition that there should be provision in the neighbourhood for children of other denominations and that all books in such schools should be sanctioned by the board. No agreement was reached before Morley was succeeded by the conservative, Gerald Balfour, who ended the negotiations.[25] No change, therefore, occurred in McAlister's lifetime.

When preparations were being made by the Belfast City Council to appoint an attendance committee, which would in turn appoint officers to visit the schools, and the names of the five members who would work alongside five chosen by the

25 Akenson, *Irish education experiment*, 360–70.

commissioners in Dublin were being mentioned, McAlister wrote to the council. Remarking that the secular and religious instruction of children were so inseparable as to require their simultaneous progress, he felt it his duty, as no Catholic was a member of the council, to appeal to it to appoint to the attendance committee and in proportion to their numbers Catholics in whom he could have confidence. The council replied that it accepted the suggestion of having a proportionate number of Catholics on the attendance committee but, as its appointments were to be made from its own numbers, suggested that the bishop submit the names of two or three members whom the commissioners might appoint. McAlister replied that he planned to contact the commissioners and would be happy to submit names, if they were willing to agree to such an appointment.[26]

The commissioners duly appointed three Catholics to the attendance committee which ensured a reasonable proportion. But the bishop took offence because two of the three were priests about whose nomination he had not been consulted. They then resigned, presumably under pressure from him, and the *Irish News* claimed that the commissioners' action was 'unbecoming and discreditable'.[27] The Catholics as a result of McAlister's attitude were therefore left under-represented on the committee.

Trouble soon broke out over the membership of the Belfast attendance committee. Objections were raised to the town clerk being given an additional salary as secretary to it, and to the choice of two inspectors who did not reside in the town. Three members resigned.[28] A Catholic layman joined the committee. Despite this friction the average attendance of those on the rolls in the Belfast schools had increased by December 1894 from 70 to 77 per cent.[29] But the general increase in attendance throughout the country of those enrolled in schools increased

26 IN, 3 Oct. 1893. 27 Ibid., 22 Dec. 1893. 28 Ibid., 2 Feb. 1894.
29 Ibid., 2 Mar. 1895.

very little in the first six years after the introduction of compulsion.[30]

Cardinal Logue speaking in Cookstown shortly after the act took effect declared that he had never found compulsion necessary and did not think it useful. Disbelieving in coercion even for children, he predicted that the act would be a failure, and asserted that, if the money that was spent on school attendance officers were spent on providing clothing for poor children, far more children would go to school voluntarily than would ever go when compelled to do so by law.[31]

The commissioners of national education soon found flaws in the legislation. In a minute in their report for 1893 they complained that the only source of income for the expenses of the attendance committees was to be derived from local rates, but if the local authorities did not provide such funds, the commissioners had no power to compel them to do so.[32]

The commissioners also bore out some of the fears that had been expressed by Sexton and his colleagues in parliament. They admitted that they encountered difficulties in dealing with local authorities, and mentioned the situation in Derry as an example. There the local authorities, having fixed the number of members on the attendance committee at ten, appointed five Protestants, none of whom were patrons or managers. Yet Catholics accounted for 55 per cent of the population. As there were only three Catholic managers or patrons in Derry City, the Catholic proportion of 55 per cent of the population would end up with only 30 per cent of the representation on the committee, if the commissioners were to appoint them. The danger, therefore, arose of such appointments provoking sectarian animosity, as the committees decided whether non-national schools were 'effi-

30 Akenson, *Irish Education experiment*, 346. Akenson, quoting from official reports states that the average percentage of daily attendance of those enrolled in schools was 63.1 in 1894. By 1899 it had increased to 64.5 but in 1900 was 62.0. 31 IC, 24 Feb. 1894. 32 Sixtieth report of the commissioners of national education [C7457], H. C. 1894, xxx, pt. II, 8–11.

cient', whether children not attending school were receiving suit-able elementary education, whether excuses for non-attendance were 'reasonable' and whether it was 'expedient' to take proceed-ings in the case of non-attendance. The commissioners noted that of the 88 places where school attendance committees had been appointed the act was only in full operation in 45 of them. But they pointed out that where the act was enforced, the inspec-tors, managers and teachers were convinced that it had proved beneficial and increased attendances.

Subsequent amendments to the act removed the obligation to ensure that at least half the members of the attendance com-mittee were patrons or managers to avoid giving disproportionate representation to any denomination. The act was also adjusted to take account of other refinements of excuses for non-attendance.[33] By March 1895 when McAlister died, the act had not impinged in any serious way on the Catholic community in his diocese, and subsequently never bore out the apprehension or even dread which he and some of his colleagues had entertained about it.

II

Another educational issue which troubled the bishops was the claim by teachers to have some security of tenure rather than be subject to dismissal by a decision of the manager alone. Teachers of all denominations were anxious about the power which man-agers enjoyed in this area and believed that it had not always been exercised with rigorous justice. In the 1880s discussions began to take place on managerial authority at teachers' con-gresses. After one such congress of the Dundalk association in 1887 a deputation approached Archbishop Logue about the establishment of a court of inquiry into any case of alleged

---

33 Ibid., 11.

arbitrary dismissal. Logue agreed that any teacher who was served with the three months notice of dismissal and felt aggrieved about it should contact him and the case would be investigated. That arrangement worked smoothly and during the next few years no case of unjust dismissal occurred in the archdiocese of Armagh.[34] In 1892 a deputation from the Catholic teachers of the Belfast district met Bishop McAlister to seek a similar guarantee and were assured by him that he would permit no injustice to be done to a deserving teacher in his diocese.[35]

Teachers in other parts of the country did not receive such assurances, and demands for protection from unfair dismissal by managers became more insistent. Some clergy interpreted the teachers' demands as an attack on the managerial system and, therefore, on their own authority and pastoral responsibility towards the pupils. Cardinal Logue believed that some of the teachers were opposed to the managerial system as such. He feared that there was 'an inner clique who are anything but friendly to religious interests, and they are spurred on by some of the more intemperate characters among the Parnellites'.[36] The anti-clericalism that existed within Parnellism was being used to diminish or destroy clerical involvement in the national schools.

At a meeting of the clergy of the diocese of Clogher in September 1894 resolutions similar to those already endorsed by the clergy of Armagh were passed protesting against 'the

34 IN, 17 Sept. 1894.   **35** Ibid., 6 Sept. 1894. In Jan. 1892 Protestant and Catholic managers of schools in Belfast held a public meeting to complain to the commissioners of national education about alterations and additions to the programmes of instruction in the national schools. They claimed that changes recently introduced had made the work of the pupils excessive, had distracted the teachers and could not be reasonably executed in poorly equipped Irish schools. They objected to new arrangements about standards required at certain levels in writing, needlework, sewing, music, geometry, geography, book-keeping and grammar, and requested that inspectors should have had experience as teachers. (IN, 22 Jan. 1892)   **36** Logue to Kirby, 24 Mar. 1894, AICR.

dangerous and mischievous agitation of a section' of the teachers concerning their managerial authority which was the only guarantee Catholic people had that their children's education would not be anti-Catholic. The clergy maintained that the object of many of those involved in the agitation was not merely to prevent abuses but to transfer the appointment and dismissal of teachers to the state. Exhorting the Catholic teachers of the diocese to dissociate themselves from that movement, they insisted that, if clerical managers were guilty of any abuse, it was that of overlooking the shortcomings of teachers rather than dismissing them capriciously. The right of appeal to the bishop of the diocese protected the teachers from injustice.[37]

The subject was raised at the annual meeting of the teachers of the North of Ireland at Warrenpoint in September. The chairman, while admitting that the managers had 'at all times been their best friends' and had won many improvements for them, pointed out that the desire for protection was something that was shared by prince and peasant. He praised the steps taken by some bishops and in particular by Cardinal Logue who had forbidden managers to dismiss teachers without submitting to him sufficient reasons for taking that step. A resolution was proposed and passed unanimously calling for every teacher in the country to be 'secured from the danger of unjust dismissal'. A Protestant officer, who proposed the resolution, pointed out that the Catholic teachers in some dioceses had obtained that security when their bishops had constituted themselves a court of appeal. He congratulated the Catholics on obtaining that right, but as it was impossible for many Protestants to have a similar court of appeal, he suggested that the commissioners of national education should establish a court of appeal for the protection of those who needed it. He claimed that the system of managerial authority was a grievance, 'for if there had never been a case of unjust dismissal, that one man should have

37 IN, 10 Sept. 1894.

another's liberty in his hands and be able to dismiss him without any reason, was not the spirit of the nineteenth century'. However, there had been cases of hardship inflicted by managers, both lay and clerical, and hence the need for implementing their resolution. He admitted that dismissal was justified, if the teacher were inefficient or had not a good moral character, but, if no such charges were made, the teacher was entitled to security of tenure.[38]

At their autumn meeting three weeks later the bishops addressed the question. In their subsequent statement they expressed regret that some prominent members of the teachers' organization had tried to 'effect important changes in the rules of the National Education Board subversive of the legitimate authority of the managers of schools'. They then explained that they regarded the rights of managers to appoint and dismiss teachers 'as a matter intimately and essentially connected with that control over education in its moral and religious aspects which it is their right, and, therefore, their duty to maintain'. The bishops responded to the situation by resolving to confirm the practice which had been widely applied, whereby managers could not dismiss teachers until they had obtained their bishop's permission to do so. They concluded their resolutions by ordering that a copy of them should be sent to the Chief Secretary and to the commissioners of national education – an indication of how jealously they were determined to safeguard the rights of managers.[39]

Cardinal Logue was confident that this firm response to the agitation about the managerial system would silence the critics of clerical control of the national schools. He confided to Archbishop Kirby:

> I trust it will put an end to the dangerous agitation of the
> teachers. If they now persist the end of their agitation will
> become manifest and it will be the duty of the Bishops to deal

38 Ibid., 17 Sept. 1894.   **39** Ibid., 12 Oct. 1894.

firmly with the Catholic Teachers. The fact I fear is that the teachers are spurred on by the anticlerical Parnellite party.[40]

The official declaration by all the bishops, that priests could not dismiss a teacher without submitting the case to them for their examination and agreement, assuaged the anxieties and concerns of the Catholic teachers for a time. Parish priests who might have been tempted to dismiss teachers became much more reluctant to take such action knowing that their reasons for doing so would be carefully scrutinized by the bishops and would have to be very convincing.

III

McAlister's special interest in intermediate education lay in the development of St Malachy's College. Since 1878 secondary or intermediate schools could avail of state exhibitions and prizes and receive premiums based on the results obtained at public examinations. Praising the opportunities afforded by St Malachy's at a prize-giving ceremony, he assured parents that their children were being prepared for the professions 'without being exposed to any of the dangers that attend the frequenting of any purely secular or Godless institution'. The two ends of Catholic education – preparation for an earthly career and a career in the next world – were always kept in view. In 1887 the college had 60 boarders and 146 day-boys.[41] He regretted that the college was still in debt and encouraged parents to support it.[42] He also regretted the loss of a large part of the grounds to the adjoining prison, which he was powerless to resist.

The University Education Act of 1879 which led to the establishment of the Royal University, an examining body with power

---

40 Logue to Kirby, 14 Oct. 1894, AICR. The Parnellite paper, the *Irish Daily Independent*, argued that the bishops' role as a court of appeal was completely unsatisfactory as bishops tended to side with managers for fear of undermining their authority. 41 *Relatio status dioecesis*, 1888, DCDA. 42 IN, 28 Nov. 1893.

to grant degrees, allowed students at intermediate schools to sit for university examinations. Bishop Dorrian had hoped to obtain some of the fellowships of the Royal University for St Malachy's College to enhance its status and also to make it an institution of higher education. Though he was disappointed in his quest, he encouraged students at the college to sit for examinations at the Royal University. Aspirants to the priesthood sat for these examinations before proceeding to Maynooth or other seminaries for courses in theology. But McAlister, who disliked and distrusted the Royal system, discontinued this practice. He ordered his students to move to Maynooth after the equivalent of one course in Arts and did not allow them to sit for degree examinations. He thereby deprived some of them of the opportunity of obtaining a degree.[43]

IV

The concern for boys and girls committed to reformatories and industrial schools was partly responsible for the opposition shown by McAlister and the Catholic community of Belfast to the Belfast Corporation (Lunatic Asylums, etc.) bill in 1892.

The lunatic asylum which served the city and Co. Antrim was overcrowded, and, as the population of Belfast increased, the corporation decided that more accommodation was necessary. It submitted a private bill to parliament which proposed to separate Belfast from Co. Antrim; the county would have its own asylum at Holywell, near Antrim town, and the asylum in Belfast would come under the control of the corporation instead of the grand jury, which had hitherto been responsible to a department of state in Dublin known as the Board of Control. The corporation would also commit children to the reformatories and industrial schools, and make a financial contribution to their upkeep.

43 Rogers, St Malachy's College, Belfast 1833–1933 in *The Collegian* (1933) 13–29.

When it was debated in the House of Commons in February 1892 Thomas Sexton, the member for West Belfast, immediately raised objections to it, basing his arguments on his distrust of the corporation's willingness to act fairly towards Catholics. These objections were repeated by both McAlister and other opponents of the bill. Maintaining that the wards of Belfast were so drawn as to exclude Catholics from representation on the corporation, Sexton complained that that body would be empowered to nominate twelve of the eighteen governors of the asylum. Furthermore, the separation of Belfast from Co. Antrim should have been carried out by the lord lieutenant who should also have had the right to nominate half of the governors. Sexton took exception as well to the expenditure involved in having two asylums with two staffs instead of one.[44]

Two Protestant members went further than Sexton in excoriating the corporation for its injustice to the Catholic minority in the city. Edmond Knox, MP for West Cavan, claimed that the bill proposed 'to set up a religious tyranny over the Catholic minority' and invited the house to pause before it 'set up an engine of religious persecution'. Jeremiah Jordan, MP for West Clare, declared that 'in their narrow self-importance the Protestants of Belfast refuse the least justice to their Catholic fellow-townsmen'.[45]

A meeting of Catholic ratepayers was held in St Mary's Hall on 20 March to voice objections to the bill. Seven priests and several prominent laymen were present. The chairman, Dr Alexander Dempsey, explained that under the existing regulations the corporation nominated six of the governors of the asylum, the grand jury nominated six and the Lord Lieutenant nominated twelve. That proportion should have been sufficient for the corporation and better medical care could be provided for the patients in one large institution rather then in two.

44 Hansard, (Fourth Series), I, 1334–8 (26 Feb. 1892). 45 Ibid., 1348–51 (26 Feb. 1892), 1596–7 (1 Mar. 1892).

Under the bill the town council would have the option of con-
tributing a certain sum to the industrial schools, and, when it
obtained control of them, might possibly contribute less than it
was obliged to do under the existing system. The council could
refuse to increase the number of certificates issued to the
Catholic industrial schools and even use its influence to prevent
children being sent to them. William McCormick explained
that, since Catholic interests had been entirely ignored by the
corporation until then, they were bound to view the prospect of
placing themselves 'in any way in the hands of a body of gentlemen who have not been conspicuous for their attention in
any degree to their interests as Catholic ratepayers . . . with a
feeling of the utmost distrust'. He also voiced his fear that the
town council would refuse to take children from outside the city
boundary into the industrial schools. A petition expressing
opposition to the extension of the corporation's power over the
asylum and industrial schools was drawn up and Thomas Sexton
was called upon to champion their views in parliament.[46]

The bill was submitted to a select committee of seven members of the House of Commons which met in London. Among
its leading members was Sexton, who duly prompted the
Catholics who appeared before it to highlight their fears and
anxieties about it. Sexton himself had already referred to the
underemployment of Catholics in various offices controlled by
the corporation and allied bodies, noting their religion and
salaries. Charles McLorinan, a prominent Catholic solicitor,
who appeared before the committee stressed that Catholics
numbered 70,000 out of a population of 270,000 and
expressed his fear that the corporation, which took a narrower
view of its obligations than the grand jury, might lower the
grant to the industrial school run by the Sisters of Mercy.[47]

46 IN, 21 Mar. 1892.   47 McLorinan informed the committee that the 10
aldermen and 30 councillors of the corporation, who were Protestant, were
unpaid. He submitted a list of public officials by religious denomination and

McAlister addressed the committee on 12 May. He emphasized that he did not object to the corporation because its
members were Protestant 'but on account of the treatment they
are giving us' as they tried 'to use a common word, to boycott
us in every direction'. He explained that he was one of the three
Catholic governors of the asylum[48] who owed their appointment to the lord lieutenant. Predicting that elective county
government would soon be established in Ireland, he regarded
the possibility of 'extensive financial arrangements' between
Belfast and Counties Antrim and Down which would be
binding in the future as 'most undesirable, not to say intoler-
able'. The alteration of the 'existing gerrymandered wards'
which would allow Catholics to have 'a proportionate representation' on the town council should precede the passing of the
bill. Reminding the committee that in 1887 a royal commission
had proposed that justices of the peace in Belfast should be
excluded from the bench and noting that the Catholics had no

salary: the town clerk (£2,300), accountant (£600) the 14 clerks and assistants
to the town clerk and accountant (£1,680), the town surveyor (£800) and the
8 assistants (£1,180), the superintendent of the fire brigade and 4 inspectors
(£720), the solicitors for the petty sessions (£350), the health superintendent
(£500) and his 3 assistants (£550), the clerk of markets (£250) and his assistant inspectors (£280), the manager of the gas works (£1,000) and his 46
assistants and clerks (£5,580), the superintendent of the library (£240) and his
3 assistants (£220) and 2 superintendents of the cemetery and parks (£360).
Of these 89 were Protestant and 2 (a street inspector and a clerk of the markets) were Catholic. The 22 commissioners of the Harbour Board and their
37 employees, as principal officers and clerks, deputy harbour masters and
pilot masters were all Protestants. One water commissioner out of 16 was a
Catholic but the secretary, 6 engineers, clerks and assistants were not. Of the
22 elected poor law guardians none was a Catholic but 1 of the 22 *ex officio*
guardians was. In the workhouse 3 teachers were Protestant and 2 were
Catholic, and 40 nurses were Protestant and 1 was Catholic; all the other officers -clerk, matron, physicians, relieving officers, collectors, solicitor, medical
officers, registrars of births and deaths – were Protestant. Three of the 22 governors of the asylum were Catholics, as were 8 of the 68 attendants. The 5
physicians, clerk and matron were Protestant. None of the 11 senior officers
of the petty sessions was a Catholic. (Report from the Select Committee on
the Belfast Corporation (Lunatic Asylums etc.) Bill, 1892, 323–37. **48** The
others were Arthur Hamill, a Catholic Conservative landowner, and Dr James
Cuming, a professor at Queen's College.

confidence in the justices, he suggested that police magistrates, as in Dublin, and not the local justices of the peace should be responsible for committing children to the industrial schools.[49] To Sexton's query as to whether the conferring of the powers being sought by the town council would place the local justices of peace 'under a new temptation to partial conduct in regard to Catholics', he answered that such might be the case. Questioned as to why he thought the corporation might pay less for Catholic than for Protestant children, he answered that the only evidence he had for such a view was its past history, but he was not prepared to say that it would pay less for Catholic children in the future. When Sexton pressed the suggestion that the corporation might refuse to contribute to an industrial school, or pay a lower rate than that paid by the grand juries of Antrim and Down, or strike a differential rate and pay half a crown to Protestant industrial schools and two shillings or less to Catholic schools, he conceded that it would have the power to do so. County Antrim had guaranteed a loan of £5,000 from the Board of Works to a Catholic industrial school, but the bill did not make provision for the corporation to take its share of the guarantee.

McAlister also claimed that the governors had not decided in 1888 whether to enlarge the asylum or to build an 'auxiliary institution'. Those who favoured the erection of a new building were the members of the corporation who wanted to get control of the premises in Belfast and would then have eleven or twelve rather than six of the twenty-two governors. Drawing attention to the importance of having Catholic attendants at the asylum and workhouse (which also had a large proportion of 'ordinary and insane paupers'), who could alert the chaplain to the need to administer the sacraments to the dying, he

---

49 Industrial schools provided education for children who had been committed by court order and for a few children from broken homes or who had lost one or both parents.

expressed reasonable satisfaction with the number of Catholic attendants at the asylum – fourteen – but dissatisfaction with the number of Catholic nurses at the workhouse – one out of forty-two.[50] If the scheme proposed in the bill were to be carried out, he suggested that the corporation should nominate three-quarters of the local governors and that Catholic ratepayers should be allowed to nominate one-quarter with the lord lieutenant taking the religious complexion of the city into account when appointing the others; out of twenty-two governors five or six would be Catholics, eight or nine representatives of the Corporation and the remainder would be chosen by the viceroy.[51]

Two priests, Daniel McCashin and James Hamill, who were the corresponding managers of the male and female industrial schools, also gave evidence. Expressing satisfaction with the financial support enjoyed by his school from the grand juries of Antrim and Down, McCashin pointed out that there was a danger of the town council taking a different course, and argued that its whole tendency had been 'so much in the direction of excluding and crippling Catholics that when they got any more direct power they would use it in that same direction'.[52] Hamill explained that the two Catholic industrial schools were certified to accommodate 260 children and the four Protestant schools to accommodate 510 children. Of the 144 in his female school, 127 were committed in Belfast, one in Dublin and the others in Antrim and Down. He complained about the minuscule proportions of Catholic teachers and nurses in the workhouse where 1,326 of the 2,642 inmates were Catholics, and having regard to the corporation's 'persistent and systematic treatment of Catholics' for twenty-five years he was afraid that it would

50 These figures differ slightly from those supplied by Charles McLorinan. McLorinan claimed that 8 of the 68 attendants at the asylum were Catholics and one of the 41 nurses was a Catholic. **51** Report from the Select Committee on the Belfast Corporation (Lunatic Asylums etc.) Bill, 1892, 357–74. **52** Ibid., 380–2.

refuse grants to their schools.[53] William McCormick, a Catholic estate agent, who also gave evidence to the committee, claimed that twelve members of the corporation were local justices of the peace and thirteen others had been members. It was therefore very desirable that the committals to the industrial schools should be made by police magistrates rather than by those who had been or were members of the corporation.[54]

Some of the objections of the Catholics to parts of the bill were duly accepted. The corporation was not authorized to assume financial control over the expenditure of the industrial schools, and was not permitted to vest the asylum in its own body. Like all others in Ireland it was vested in the board of control in Dublin. The corporation withdrew the clause by which it proposed to nominate two-thirds of the governors: one half was to be appointed locally and the other half by the lord lieutenant. Sexton declared himself satisfied with the alterations, and, presumably, the bishop and the others who had given evidence before the select committee shared his satisfaction.

A proposal to increase provision for the mentally handicapped might seem at first sight an extremely strange issue for McAlister, some of his laity and members of the Irish parliamentary party to use against the Belfast Corporation. But the management of the asylum, and especially the employment of Catholic nursing staff who would be always be ready to summon chaplains to attend the sick and dying caused the bishop and priests some anxiety. They were also keen to have more Catholic governors to represent their share of the population of the city. But the crucial element in the bishop's opposition to the bill was the control which it might afford to the corporation over the industrial schools. He feared that, if the members or past members of the corporation were given more charge over the committals of children and grants towards their maintenance, they might use those powers

---

53 Ibid., 383–405. 54 Ibid., 374–80.

to the detriment of the Catholic body. He and his friends were therefore determined to close all loopholes in the legislation lest any misuse of power could occur. Distrust of the corporation was the root cause of Catholic opposition to the bill.

McAlister was also a governor of the asylum at Downpatrick, where much less friction seems to have arisen between the governors and the ecclesiastical authorities. But when William Johnston, MP, the outspoken Orangeman and former governor, was not reappointed by the lord lieutenant, he complained that his place had been taken by the bishop. McAlister repudiated the claim in a public letter in which he rather generously admitted to having had 'the greatest respect for Mr Johnston, and admired the bold and straightforward way in which he gave expression to the extreme views which he held on religion, temperance and politics' but expressed surprise that Johnston had not seen his name on the list of governors in previous years. He added that the new government had had 'the courage to appoint a few of its own supporters to be governors of that asylum', and implied that Johnston should have found the grounds for his exclusion in that policy.[55] Compared to the disputes over the Belfast asylum this was a very minor spat.

V

Distrust also soured relations between boards of guardians, staff at workhouses and Catholic clergy. The religious denomination of teachers in the workhouse schools afforded frequent opportunities for disputes. The boards of guardians, who managed the workhouses, were chosen by the ratepayers; justices of the peace were *ex officio* members. All the boards in the diocese of Down and Connor had Protestant majorities.

During Bishop Dorrian's episcopate quarrels between guardians and chaplains had taken place, and some of these

55 IN, 26 Jan. 1893.

continued after Dorrian's death. Michael McConvey, the parish priest of Newtownards, who had previously complained about the treatment of Catholic children during religious instruction and about his salary in proportion to that of clergy of other denominations, continued to pursue complaints during McAlister's episcopate. He took exception to the state of the room in which he was permitted to celebrate Mass. The matron consented to re-arrange some of the furnishings of the room and, though the master apologized, he claimed that McConvey was merely seeking an excuse to embarrass him.[56]

At Downpatrick the teachers were evenly divided in religious terms: the master of the male school was a Catholic and the mistress of the female school was a Protestant. When the master resigned the guardians decided to amalgamate the schools under the control of the mistress. Despite the appeal of the Catholic chaplain to the Local Government Board in Dublin, the guardians held firm. Though it was pointed out that only two resident Catholic officials had held office in the workhouse, no change occurred.[57]

When the mistress retired a few years later a Catholic applicant, regarded as the most suitable, was not appointed. Of the twenty-one children in the school three were Anglicans, three Presbyterians and fifteen Catholics. To cater for the religious education of the Catholic majority a catechist was provided, but the expected salary of fifteen pounds per annum was reduced to eight.[58]

The *Northern Whig* noted with regret that the board of guardians at Lisburn had no Catholic members even though there were respectable Catholic traders and others well qualified for office in the district. However, religious antagonisms prevented their being elected.[59] The kind of dispute which

---

56 MN, 15 Nov. 1886. **57** Ibid., 28 Nov. 1887, 13 Mar. 1888.
58 Ibid., 2 May, 14 June 1892. **59** NW, 12 Sept. 1888, 2 June 1889.

occurred at Magherafelt, when nuns were refused permission to teach religion in the workhouse, did not occur at Lisburn.[60]

James O'Kane, the chaplain at Belfast workhouse, had several disputes with the officials and their employers, the guardians. He objected to the absence or virtual absence of Catholic nurses who would understand and be sympathetic to the religious requirements of Catholic patients and who would summon a priest when his ministration was required. He pointed out that only three of the ninety-four employees at the workhouse were Catholics, and claimed that two of the three were there by necessity, as they were teachers.[61] An advertisement for an assistant teacher a year later provoked O'Kane to object again to practices at the workhouse. He wrote to say that in the notice in the newspaper a Presbyterian was required to assist in the female school. He explained that there were then in the female school one principal and two assistants. Of the 142 children in the school, 85 were Catholics. If a Presbyterian were appointed, 29 Presbyterian children would have two teachers to care for their religious education and 85 Catholic children would have only one. O'Kane's letter was heeded and the advertisement for the teacher made no reference to religion.[62]

Disputes arose from time to time about the religious denomination of children in the workhouse. Catholic chaplains accused the guardians of trying to have children of doubtful religious background brought up as Protestants. In the Belfast workhouse a boy named Patrick McCallum asked to be registered as a Catholic. The guardians refused, as he had been educated for seven years in the workhouse as a Protestant, and, when questioned by a committee, had given such incoherent answers that they did not feel justified in changing his registration. However, James O'Kane, the chaplain, wrote to the Local Government Board, which replied that unless the medical officer was prepared

60 MN, 18 Sept. 1891. **61** IN, 7, 11 May 1892. **62** Ibid., 29 Nov. 1893.

to certify that the boy was of unsound mind, the guardians were obliged to accede to his request.[63]

The Ballycastle board of guardians was ordered by the Local Government Board to bring back to the workhouse a Catholic child whom they had sent out to a Protestant family and who would have been reared as a Protestant.[64]

McAlister himself made a public comment about practices obtaining in the Belfast workhouse, which were not related to sectarian disputes. He complained that the board of governors of the Belfast district asylum, motivated by a desire to give control of the asylum to the corporation, had adopted new arrangements for the accommodation of the insane which still left 400 people who suffered from insanity in the Belfast workhouse. He quoted extensively from the reports of inspectors on the care of the insane in the workhouse in 1890. The inspectors disapproved of the policy of confining many of the insane to bed merely to avoid 'the trouble of attending them when up'. Many epileptics were kept in bed because they suffered from frequent fits, and 'mechanical restraint would appear to be made use of indiscriminately in many instances without sufficient reason for its use'. Improvements were reported at the inspection of 1892, especially in the case of mechanical restraint but too many epileptics were still being confined to bed.

McAlister explained that he was not blaming the guardians of the workhouse, who, he believed, would have intervened to protect the sufferers had they known about them. But he stressed that 'workhouses were not suited to the treatment of the insane and in the interests of humanity they ought to be placed in properly equipped asylums where they would secure the care and attention suitable to their helpless state'. He had, therefore, voted against the scheme which proposed to leave 400 insane poor for an indefinite period in the workhouse, and

63 MN, 15 Nov. 1893.   **64** Ibid., 31 Mar. 1890.

felt that, as the asylum was being enlarged, they should be removed from their unsuitable surroundings. On the grounds of humanity he appealed for the support of the press 'of all shades of politics'.[65]

The tensions that occurred over religious issues in the work-houses merely reflected the animosities and ill-feeling prevailing in society. The antagonisms and bitterness generated by the campaign for, and resistance to, Home Rule greatly exacerbated that discord.

65 IN, 11 Oct. 1893.

Chapter Five

Conflict with the Passionists

THROUGHOUT HIS ENTIRE episcopate McAlister carried on an implacable and unyielding dispute with the religious order of the Passionists. It was a dispute he inherited but which he could easily have settled: however, instead of compromising in a spirit of goodwill he prolonged and intensified the quarrel, leaving relations with the only male religious order in the diocese more strained and inimical than he had found them.

In 1868 Bishop Dorrian invited the Passionists to establish a house and church in Belfast. In that decade the population of the town was growing rapidly and the Catholic portion of it increased from 41,406 in 1861 (almost 34 per cent of the total) to 55,575 in 1871.[1] Though two Catholic churches, St Peter's and the new St Mary's were opened in the 1860s, provision for the pastoral care of those settling in the suburbs at Ardoyne and Ligoniel had still to be made. Consequently, Dorrian in an attempt to provide that care invited the Passionists to take up residence at Ardoyne and sold them a piece of ground which he owned in that area. He envisaged their working in that district in much the same way as the curates of his own quasi-parishes, rather than as a religious order with wider obligations and responsibilities. In their willingness to accept his offer to establish a house in Belfast, the Passionists submitted to conditions which

---

1 Budge & O'Leary, *Belfast, approach to crisis*, 32.

they soon came to regret: the superior was to be accountable to the bishop as a quasi-pastor and, when removed or changed, his successor was to be presented to the bishop; members of the order were not to carry out any function outside their district without the bishop's permission; the bishop was to enjoy the right of ordering general collections in their church (in practice he took one third of their monthly and voluntary collections); they were not allowed to 'quest' or seek alms outside their district without the bishop's permission and then only during the time assigned to them.[2] In 1869 the Passionists established a temporary church and set to work in the Ardoyne and Ligoniel areas. But they resented the restrictions Dorrian had placed on them, especially in regard to collections and questing, and his limitation of faculties for hearing confessions to four of their number. They were also hampered by the bishop's refusal to allow them to make public appeals for money to replace their temporary church,[3] which he justified on the grounds that the Catholics of Belfast had too many other debts to pay off before they could incur a further one. In 1886 McAlister inherited a situation where a religious order felt aggrieved at its treatment by his predecessor for the previous eighteen years.

Archbishop Persico called at Ardoyne during his visit to Belfast in August 1887 and was given a memorandum by a former superior detailing the frustrations experienced by the Passionists during Dorrian's episcopate, especially the repeated postponements of permission to build a new church. Pointing out that they served 1,600 people at Ardoyne and 1,100 at Ligoniel in unsatisfactory buildings and could find work for eight or ten confessors for their own people and for those from other parts of Belfast who came to them, instead of the four they were allowed, Alphonsus O'Neill maintained that no such

2 Memorandum of Eugenius Martorelli to Propaganda, 1888, APF, SC 43, f 107r.   3 This wooden church, erected in 1869, was only ninety feet long by twenty-nine feet wide.

restrictions were placed on houses of their order in England, Ireland, Scotland or America.[4] Persico does not seem to have taken any action to rectify the situation.

In the second year of McAlister's episcopate relations deteriorated further. When none of the Passionists were present at the diocesan conference on 31 August 1887, McAlister's vicar general called at their house and advised the superior to write to the bishop to explain why they were absent. The bishop apparently insisted in his reply that all members of the community should be available to attend the conferences, and, rather than leave Ardoyne to conduct missions in other parishes, should spend all their time in pastoral work at home. The superior forwarded this letter to the provincial in London, pointing out that they had only 2,600 Catholics in their care, while some curates had between 3,000 and 4,000 Catholics, and in some cases 5,000 Catholics to look after.[5] He suggested that the time had come for the Passionists to stand up for their rights by appealing to Rome, if necessary, and recalled that their church was 'in a wretched state ... and in so far as the Bishop is concerned we are to remain in this crippled and well-nigh helpless state'.[6]

Vincent Grogan, the provincial in London, wrote to McAlister asking that his colleagues at Ardoyne be given proper recognition as a religious order and explaining that in their houses in England and Scotland only the superior or his substitute attended the conferences. He also complained about the refusal of faculties to more than four of their priests to hear confessions, and about the vague promises and postponements with which his predecessor had responded to their requests to replace their unsafe temporary church.[7] Grogan apparently found the

4 O'Neill to Persico, 5 Aug. 1887, PCA, 5/2/1/2. **5** According to McAlister's census in 1888 each priest in St Peter's parish had more than 3,000 and in St Patrick's parish a little less than 3,000. In St Paul's, St Malachy's and St Mary's the figure was one to more than 1,000 and in St Joseph's 1:1,000. **6** Anthony Carroll to Vincent Grogan, n.d. PCA 5/2/1/3). **7** Grogan to McAlister, 26 Sept. 1887, APF, SC (Irlanda) 42, bishop's reply unsatisfactory as it did not do him 'the justice of admitting the honesty or rectitude' of his motives.[8] He therefore wrote again stressing that all the Passionists wanted was a recognition of their rights and privileges as an exempt religious community. Quoting official documents about their rights to be recognized as confessors and their freedom from the obligation to attend conferences (except in the case of the rector who had pastoral care) he appealed for the same treatment from the bishop of Down and Connor as they received in London, Glasgow, Liverpool and elsewhere.[9]

The plea for a recognition of rights and privileges seems only to have hardened the bishop's resolve. He obviously consulted a canonist about the technicalities of the Passionists' claims and argued in his reply that their institute was not a regular order whose members took solemn vows but a religious congregation, whose members required approbation and jurisdiction from the local bishop. He then referred to the sexual immorality of which one of their members had been guilty, and to bitter feelings which had been aroused among the people by anonymous letters in the press in reference to the rebuilding of their church and by allusions to the same from the altar at Ardoyne. Charging that the 'unpleasant relations' had originated with themselves, he therefore felt 'constrained in the interests of religion not to accede' to their demands.[10]

In fact the dispute had become angrier when McAlister refused faculties to officiate as a confessor to a fifth priest at Ardoyne and told the one to whom he gave faculties that their renewal depended on his attending the diocesan conferences during the following year.[11] The provincial of the Passionists, exasperated by the bishops general hostility and stung by his

ff 855r–859r. **8** In a letter possibly dated 21 Nov. 1887 Anthony Carroll told Grogan that McAlister was 'awfully sore on the letter you sent him'. (PCA 5/2/1/5/) **9** Grogan to McAlister (copy) 23 Jan. 1888, PCA 5/2/1/8. **10** McAlister to Vincent Grogan, 6 Feb. 1888, PCA, 5/2/1/10. **11** APF, SC (Irlanda) 43, ff 107r–135r.

challenge to the canonical status of the order, informed him that, 'to the same extent as all other Regulars they were exempt from episcopal authority', that, as he was denying them the privileges to which, as regulars, they were entitled, and as his treatment of the order was 'uncanonical and injurious' to their welfare, he was appealing to the Holy See.[12]

McAlister in reply accused the Passionists of having taken up a hostile position towards him and then of having aggravated it by their letters to him. They appeared 'blind to every interest' except that of their congregation. Arguing that they had freely chosen the conditions under which they operated, he rejected their posture of parading themselves 'as injured innocents, suffering great grievances' and insisted that he had denied them nothing which he could in conscience concede. He again questioned their claims to privileges granted by the Holy See to regular clergy.[13]

The provincial, Grogan, supplied McAlister with lengthy quotations from official documents in Latin to justify their claims to privileges, but admitted that his approach had been unsuccessful:

> Although I have taken much pains & trouble in explaining all these matters to your Lordship I see that I can gain nothing in return, but on the contrary to be accused of threatening if I suggest an appeal to the Holy See, of being hostile to the bishop if I claim the privileges of the Congregation & of *untruthfulness*, if I say that restrictions which are clearly opposed to ecclesiastical law are *arbitrary*.

He also pointed out that in Armagh there were 36 regular clergy, in Dublin 240, in Cork 43 and in Galway 10. Nonetheless, he was still prepared to settle their differences without recourse to Rome.[14] McAlister, however, was in no

---

12 Grogan to McAlister (copy), 22 Feb. 1888, APF, SC (Irlanda) 43 ff 107r–135r. 13 McAlister to Grogan, 6 Mar. 1888, PCA. 14 Grogan to

mood for conciliation. Taking up a comment of Grogan's in reply about the small number of religious in Down and Connor in contrast to the numbers in Armagh, Dublin, Cork and Galway he claimed that greater religious progress had been made in Belfast than in any of those places in the previous thirty years, and attributed it to the exertions of the diocesan clergy. The religious were anxious to enjoy the fruits of their labours but he would not 'be justified in taking the bread from the hardworking, laborious children of the diocese & giving it to strangers who have done nothing for the diocese'.[15]

The case was formally submitted to the Congregation of Propaganda on 30 April 1888. McAlister himself was in Rome in the following month and Cardinal Simeoni suggested to the consultor of the Passionists to speak to him about the dispute. But the bishop left Rome before this could be arranged.[16] Accordingly the cardinal wrote to McAlister suggesting that he make concessions in an amicable manner.[17] And Grogan, the provincial, did likewise suggesting also that their agreement be formal and written, and asking for faculties for two of his priests.[18] Propaganda also encouraged McAlister to make this concession.[19] But the bishop was determined to press his case as vigorously as he could. He replied to Rome justifying his regulation about the Passionists attending clerical conferences, claimed that their church was big enough for their purposes, repeated his charge about their responsibility for not preventing letters of complaint in the newspapers, and expressed his willingness to see their church built when his own debts of £30,000 had diminished. He also maintained that the Catholics of the town, who numbered 55,000, had ample opportunities for confession, as his own priests heard confessions for two hours each

McAlister, 9 Mar. 1888, PCA 5/2/1/5. **15** McAlister to Grogan, 18 Apr. 1888, PCA. **16** Thomas O'Connor to Grogan (?), 28 May 1888, PCA. **17** Ibid., 9 June 1888, PCA 5/2/1/20. **18** Grogan to McAlister (copy), 19 June 1888, PCA, 5/2/1/21. **19** Propaganda to McAlister, 30 July 1888 APF, N.S. 56, rubr 12, ff 204r–205v.

morning throughout the year, for four hours on Friday and Saturday evenings and in paschal time for three hours every evening. He added that he, his vicar and secretary heard confessions each Saturday for eight hours. Moreover, he had little regard for the Passionists either as directors of missions or as confessors.[20]

McAlister had summoned his clergy to a meeting to obtain their support for his submission to Rome and he enclosed a letter they sent to him after it. Signed by four vicars-general, six administrators of the quasi-parishes of Belfast and forty-five other priests, it affirmed his claim about the Catholic population of the town, about the ample opportunities for the people to confess, about the need for any new church at Ardoyne to be in keeping with the wants of the district rather than to oppress the people with debt and concluded that, if the Passionists could not accept the conditions to which they had already agreed, they should leave the diocese.[21]

The Passionist at Rome, Thomas O'Connor, who was looking after their case at Propaganda, though confident of ultimate success, reported that the congregation was 'very loath to irritate the Bishop, and the trouble caused by the Rescript of the Holy Office has had its influence in making them cautious'.[22] If, as seems likely, this interpretation was correct, McAlister was being favoured by a fortunate coincidence that bore no relation to the dispute at issue. The rescript condemning the Plan of Campaign and boycotting had been issued on 23 April 1888, and Rome had been taken aback by the hostile reaction of the Irish bishops to it and by their inaction in promulgating it. The

---

20 McAlister to Propaganda, 20 Oct. 1888, Ibid., ff 224r–246r. He explained the discrepancy in the figures for the Catholic population of Belfast by stating that according to the census of 1881 it was 59,975 and according to that carried out by the priests in 1887 it was 58,731. When the parish of Ballymacarrett was taken out of these figures the parish of Belfast had about 55,000. **21** Ibid., no date, ff 247r–148v. **22** Thomas O'Connor to Arthur Devine, 4 July 1888, PCA 5/2/1/24.

congregation of Propaganda did not wish to engage in further conflict with Irish bishops at that time. The Passionists were, therefore, unlucky in the timing of their appeal.

Either the cardinal prefect or secretary of Propaganda discussed the quarrel with the pope about the end of November 1888, for the consultor of the Passionists in Rome sent a report of a conversation with Archbishop Jacobini to his provincial in early December. Jacobini had told him that the pope did not wish to put pressure on the bishop, but would advise him to give a general permission to their colleagues at Ardoyne to hear the confessions of any sick persons who sent for them. Jacobini had added that something further might be done later, but the consultor concluded gloomily that the atmosphere in Rome in the wake of the rescript was not conducive to their cause:

> The secret of the whole matter is that the authorities here do not want to give any new cause of irritation to the Irish Bishops and this is the reason why from the beginning Propaganda declined to try the case officially or juridically, foreseeing that agreeably to all previous legislation touching the point in controversy the decision would have to be in our favour.[23]

It would seem that not only did the congregation of Propaganda not want to get further embroiled in a dispute with an Irish bishop but even the pope himself thought the time was not propitious for doing so.

However, the congregation gave a letter to Thomas O'Connor, the consultor to bring to McAlister encouraging him to allow seven or eight priests at Ardoyne to minister and hear confessions, and to facilitate the proposals to build a church. O'Connor interviewed the bishop on 14 January 1889, but the request for an extension of the faculties was refused, and

---

23 Thomas O'Connor to Vincent Grogan, 4 Dec. 1888, PCA, 5/22/1/31. The pope allegedly said *non voglio forzare il vescovo* – I do not wish to force the bishop's hand.

the Passionists were still obliged to seek permission from the priests of other parishes, if they wished to attend the sick and dying there. McAlister did agree to the building of the church,[24] but, apparently, demanded the right to decide on the precise site of it.

The dangerous condition of the temporary building had eventually forced the bishop's hand. As a result of a damaging architect's report, he, the architect and Daniel McCashin, the administrator of St Malachy's parish, who was his part-time secretary and confidant, inspected it in October 1889 and could not question the professional verdict on it.[25] Accordingly, he wrote to Propaganda giving his consent to the erection of a new church, but insisting that it should occupy the site of the old one, should be suited to the standards obtaining in the district and that the rector should help him to pay for it.[26] The cardinal prefect of Propaganda invited Thomas O'Connor in Rome to formulate conditions for an agreement about a new church, which he duly did. These stipulated that the church would belong to the diocese for the service of the people of Ardoyne but that the Passionists would have perpetual use of it, and, secondly, that it would be built on the site chosen by the architect which would allow direct communication with the house of the community.[27]

Cardinal Simeoni then wrote to McAlister proposing that he accept the conditions about ownership and use. He left the location to the bishop's judgement but emphasized the importance and convenience of placing it near the monastery on the site chosen by the architect.[28]

But the Passionists at Ardoyne, grown wary of McAlister's

---

24 O'Connor to Propaganda, registered 26 Mar. 1889, APF NS 56, rubr. 12, ff 260r–261r. **25** Anthony O'Carroll to Vincent Grogan, 26 Oct. 1889, PCA, 5/2/1/33. **26** McAlister to Propaganda, 30 Oct. 1889, APF, NS 56, rubr. 12, f 262rv. **27** O'Connor to Arthur Devine, 14 Nov. 1889, PCA 5/2/1/34. **28** Propaganda to McAlister (copy), no date, PCA, 5/2/1/30.

claims, did not want to give him any title to the church or let him have anything to do with building it. O'Connor, their agent in Rome, was nonplussed by this attitude as he feared Propaganda would then give the bishop leave to build where he liked and they would lose everything. He therefore requested his provincial to agree to accepting the bishop's right of owner-ship, provided they were guaranteed perpetual use of it.[29] The provincial then wrote to Cardinal Simeoni stating that they should build the church with the support of their friends and benefactors, on their own land and on the site chosen by the architect. As they did not wish to have pastoral charge of a parish but rather to operate as regular clergy, they were prepared to let the church belong to the diocese as long as they were granted the perpetual use of it.[30]

A few months later they explained to the bishop that they were prepared to concede to him all the rights to which he was entitled in canon law, provided they were granted perpetual use of the church as long as they remained in Ardoyne and allowed to enjoy their faculties and privileges as regulars. They then passed on to Cardinal Simeoni what they deemed to be McAlister's incomprehensible reply in which he stated that they had conveyed to him their 'final refusal of my request regarding the site of the Church, which I propose to build for the accom-modation of the people of the Ardoyne district which you occupy as administrator'.[31] The bishop subsequently explained that the church, if attached to the monastery, which was too sumptuous for the district, would be a permanent fixture, and presumably, his control over it would be diminished. Blaming them for not showing any interest in the church at Ligoniel, which also needed to be rebuilt, he concluded that the only

29 O'Connor to Vincent Grogan, 28 Nov. 1889, PCA, 5/2/1/37.
30 Vincent Grogan to Simeoni, 30 Nov. 1889, ibid., 5/2/1/39.
31 Provincial to Propaganda, 15 Nov. 1890, APF, NS 56, rubr 12, ff 268r–269r.

solution to their difficulties was that the order should leave Belfast.[32]

Frustrated by the failure or refusal of the congregation of Propaganda to take decisive action, the Passionists submitted a formal petition to the pope in January 1891. It began by listing the three points in dispute with the bishop: the site and the size of the proposed church and the conditions under which the Passionists would serve it. Recalling the promise made by Bishop Dorrian to help them build a church as soon as it was convenient and their construction of a flimsy wooden building within ten days to last for a year or two, they had responded patiently to appeals to delay their work until other churches were completed. Yet the attitude of the ecclesiastical authorities to them was revealed by the decision to cut off from their district the part where the better-off Catholics lived, and by the decision of Bishop McAlister two years previously to build another church five or six minutes walk away from theirs, and again to diminish their territory.[33] Moreover, they were accused by the bishop of instigating people to write letters to the newspapers about the wretched state of the church. And when the Provincial asked the papers not to publish such letters and encourage the people to donate to the bishop for his purposes the money they intended to subscribe for the erection of the church, his intervention was misunderstood and even interpreted as a hostile act.

Moreover, the bishop accused them of not being prepared to grant him a part of the land, which they had bought with their own money, as a site for the church. But they objected to his choice of site because he wanted to build it in front of their convent thereby obliging them to leave the convent to enter it and, if they were ever forced to leave the district, they could not realize the value of their property. Their monastery was sur-

---

32 McAlister to Propaganda, 15 Dec. 1890, Ibid., ff 270r–272v. **33** This was the Sacred Heart church on the Oldpark Road which was opened in 1890.

rounded by some 20,000 Protestants, a number of whom came with Catholic friends to their services, and as the restoration of the people of England and Ireland to the unity of the church was one of the prime objects of their founder, St Paul of the Cross, they were not asking for too much when they sought a building large enough for those who came to it and certainly larger than their present one. The bishop wished to have inserted into the deed of ownership the condition that the church would be served by the Passionists as long as they continued to be part of the parochial clergy. That would have enabled him on the day it was opened to say that they were no longer members of the parish clergy and so entrust it to other priests. Unable to comprehend the bishop's hostility, they were prepared, if permitted by the congregation of Propaganda, to undertake the construction of the building at their own expense without appealing for money in Belfast or in the diocese of Down and Connor. And though it had been said that Propaganda would not constrain the bishop, it might be asked if it could not restrain him from opposing poor religious and treating them unjustly. As he was strong and they were weak, they appealed to the pope, the defender of the oppressed, for a favourable reply to their petition. In a postscript they added that the bishop, in response to their appeal to the Holy See, had imposed a further restriction on them: hitherto they had only been forbidden to quest or seek alms in Belfast but he had recently written to the parish priests extending that prohibition to the entire diocese, thereby removing their means of livelihood.[34]

The pope did not answer this letter personally. As was customary with such practical matters he passed it to the congregation which dealt with Irish affairs. Propaganda informed McAlister that the whole question would be officially

34 Appeal to Pope, 21 June 1891, PCA 5/2/1/42 and APF, NS 56, rubr 12, ff 277r–279r.

examined at a plenary meeting of the congregation and invited his further comments. His response was to forward yet again the conditions which the Passionists had accepted from Bishop Dorrian in 1868.[35] But the general of the Passionists seemed to think McAlister was prepared to reach a compromise and passed that information to Propaganda a few months later. But despite further encouragement nothing happened.[36] Fearing perhaps that there was little hope of being allowed to build their church the community at Ardoyne raised over £500 and renovated the old one.[37]

A stalemate in the relations between the bishop and the Passionists seems then to have been reached. McAlister had resisted the advice given him by Propaganda and barring a full investigation of the issue through a special commission, there was little more the congregation could do. In view of its other and graver commitments, not least those of a political nature in Ireland relating to the land question and the Parnell split, the congregation did not wish to let itself be dragged into another Irish crisis. It probably decided that a solution would have to await the change of circumstances created by the bishop's death.

Three years later declining health forced McAlister to seek permission from Rome to have a coadjutor or assistant with right of succession appointed. Permission was granted and on 8 January 1895 the parish priests of the diocese met in Belfast to recommend three candidates to the Holy See. According to the system operating in Ireland since 1829 the names of the three candidates who obtained the most votes were forwarded to Rome together with the comments of the bishops of the province on their suitability. Rome, however, was not obliged to appoint any of them.

The three priests who obtained the most votes were Henry Henry, president of St Malachy's College, Daniel McCashin, the

35 McAlister to Propaganda, 29 Jan. 1891, APF NS 56, ff 285r–286v.
36 APF, *Acta*, 265, ff 501r–511v.   **37** IN, 28 Sept. 1894.

administrator of St Malachy's parish and Daniel O'Loan, the professor of church history at Maynooth. Henry and McCashin obtained thirteen votes each and O'Loan got ten. Other priests received a small number of votes. As the result of this ballot was published in the newspapers, the possibility of Henry or McCashin being appointed quickly became common knowledge. The Passionists, who had an immediate and pressing interest in the succession, were so deeply disturbed by the prospect of McCashin's appointment that they sent their former provincial from London to Rome to put their concerns before the congregation of Propaganda.

Fr Alfonso di Maria submitted a long letter recounting the history of their foundation, the agreement made with Bishop Dorrian, the limitation of faculties for confession to four priests and the restrictions which applied even to visiting the sick outside their district, the financial arrangements by which they had been allowed to seek alms only once in eighteen years and were obliged to give up a third of their collections to the bishop, and finally the delays about building their church. He also explained their geographical situation, their responsibility for Ligoniel and their provision from their own resources of the existing church and the donation to them of their retreat by a benefactress. Having commented on the needs of the diocese and city of Belfast, he then explained that McCashin had been 'the constant counsellor of the present as well as of the previous bishop in the rigorous measures taken against the Religious, and his hostility to them was notorious'. Henry, on the other hand, had been opposed to the oppressive policy under which they had laboured, and had anxiously desired that they would enjoy the same liberties as religious orders enjoyed in other dioceses in Ireland.

Alfonso went on to say that there was sufficient work for six religious communities in Belfast, and noted that Dublin with a similar population had twenty such communities totalling 193 priests. Cardinal Simeoni had bidden them be patient and await the arrival of a new bishop; the time was ripe for the submission of their views.[38] This letter was followed by another in which it was claimed that McCashin had said that the Passionists should never have come to Belfast to take the bread out of the mouths of the diocesan clergy.[39]

Shortly after receiving this letter the cardinal prefect wrote to Cardinal Logue inquiring further about some of the information he had received about the appointment. He also asked about the relations of the Passionists with the bishop and whether the behaviour of the prelate had been less than favourable to them.[40] Logue visited McAlister on his death bed, and duly passed on to Rome, after the bishop's death, the reply he had received. It was a repetition of all the points he had already made apart from the statement that the Passionists were already building their church with his approval. His physical weakness, however, did not affect his resolution. He concluded by insisting that, if the Passionists were not satisfied with the conditions which they had willingly accepted, he would be pleased if they left the diocese and he would reimburse them for any expenditure they had incurred.[41]

McAlister died on 26 March before a decision was made about the appointment of a coadjutor. The parish priests met again on 29 May to recommend candidates for appointment to the vacant see and again Henry and McCashin tied with fifteen votes each. O'Loan received twelve votes. The bishops of the Armagh province met on 11 June to comment on the candidates, and saw no reason to change the recommendation they had already made for the coadjutorship. On that occasion they had remarked that both Henry and McCashin possessed the

38 Alfonso di Maria to Propaganda, 10 Feb. 1895, PCA 5/2/1/44, and APF, NS 56, ff 289r–291v. **39** Ibid., ff 293r–294r. **40** Propaganda to Logue, 19 Feb. 1895, ADA. **41** Logue to Propaganda, 1 April 1895, APF, NS 56, rubr. 12, ff 295r–302r.

right talents for episcopal office, that McCashin had all the requisite qualities, that there was some basis for the charge that Henry held Parnellite views, and went on to say that the appointment of someone holding such views favourable to a political organization that was so hostile to the clergy would be very detrimental to religion and to the dignity of the episcopate. And Cardinal Logue, who had been asked to give further information on Henry's alleged Parnellism and on dissensions among the diocesan clergy connected with geography had agreed that there was some basis to the charge.

Ordinarily the preference of the bishops for McCashin would have led to his appointment. But Cardinal Vannutelli, who presented the material for deliberation by his colleagues, drew their attention to the charge of the Passionists that the late bishop had been excessively severe towards their order and that McCashin had been his constant counsellor in the rigorous measures adopted against it. He then recalled the counsels given on several occasions by the late cardinal prefect to McAlister to adopt a more conciliatory approach to the Passionists; the advice of the pope to McAlister in 1888 to give members of the order general faculties to confess the sick; the letter to the bishop from Propaganda in 1891 stating that the dispute would be examined by the congregation, when news had come from the general of the order that the bishop was disposed to reach an agreement with it. The cardinals, in short, were reminded of the exasperation and frustration caused to the officials of the congregation by McAlister's obstinate refusal to heed its counsels of moderation and tolerance. The last thing the congregation wanted was the prolongation of that unnecessary quarrel into another episcopate, and that is what McCashin's appointment threatened to produce. The cardinals therefore decided to ignore the recommendation of the bishops in McCashin's favour and recommend to the pope that Henry should be appointed. And they added to their recommendation the injunction that Henry was to accord to the Passionists or any other religious order, that might be permitted to establish a house in that diocese, the full rights of regular clergy, and to ensure that faculties for confessions were not restricted to three or four priests and that all who wished to confess, whether sick or healthy, to the regular clergy should be free to do so.[42]

The consequences of McAlister's inflexible treatment of the Passionists not only limited and frustrated the pastoral care of the congregation in Belfast but also denied episcopal succession to the confidant whom he had hoped would succeed him. He seemingly thought that yielding to the Passionists' requests would infringe his own jurisdiction and authority, and rather than allow this to happen, he was prepared to refuse them their basic rights as regular clergy and to deny his people the full and free choice of confessors which that order offered. In his determination to retain and uphold the arrangement made by Bishop Dorrian, he deprived his own people of alternative pastoral care and antagonized a religious order by attempting to treat it as part of the diocesan clergy rather than permit it to enjoy the privileges and exemptions granted to it by the Holy See.

Henry Henry was appointed bishop of Down and Connor in August 1895, just over four months after McAlister's death and held that office until March 1908. In accordance with the instructions of Propaganda he removed his predecessor's restrictions on the Passionists. They ceased to have responsibility for Ligoniel, which became a separate parish in 1896, and were enabled to concentrate all their energies on Ardoyne, where their church was blessed and opened in 1902.

42 APF, *Acta* 265, ff 501r–511v.

Chapter Six

Pastoral developments

THE CATHOLIC POPULATION of the diocese during McAlister's episcopate hovered around 145,000. He himself in his report to Rome in 1888 put the figure at 140,314, listing the numbers in each parish. As extrapolated from the census of 1881 the Catholic population was 149,583; according to the census of 1891 it was 146,319. The population presumably increased between 1887, when the bishop's census was taken, and 1891. The census takers were also more likely to be accurate than the clergy. The figure given by the census of 1891 is almost identical with that of 1861. In the intervening years the diocese had grown but then declined again until 1901.

Belfast accounted for more than a third of the diocesan population. But the Catholic percentage of the population of the town had declined since 1861. In that year it stood at almost 34 per cent. Though the decade of the 1860s witnessed the biggest increase in the size of the town during the nineteenth century, the Catholic percentage of it dropped. In 1871 that percentage was slightly under 32; in 1881 it was slightly under 29 and by 1891 was just above 26. The migration of Catholics from the rural parts of Down and Connor, and of Ulster generally to Belfast had slowed down, but during the years 1886 to 1895 the Catholic population of Belfast continued to increase.

By the 1880s a small number of Catholics had become prosperous and rich. The Hughes family employed 150 men in their bakeries and William Ross had 600 men and women in his mills. John Hamill was an extensive landowner. Some 10 per cent of doctors and lawyers were Catholic. In 1864 Bishop Dorrian estimated that between these were seventy or eighty or ninety Catholics with capital ranging from £2,000 to £5,000 who could spare £100 out of their income 'without injuring their family prospects or interfering with their work'.[1] Some of these had made their money as successful shopkeepers and, especially, as publicans; Catholics supplied alcohol to the Protestants of the town as well as to their co-religionists and, in consequence, their livelihoods in some districts suffered severely in times of civil disturbance. Catholics also serviced their own community as minor tradesmen and artisans, but the majority earned a living as unskilled workers, labourers, domestic servants and dockers. To the Protestant-owned shipbuilding, engineering, linen and textile works they supplied mostly small minorities of the work-force. An exception was the Combe, Barbour & Combe foundry where they represented forty per cent of the workers; in Ewart's mill, which employed 3,000 they accounted for twenty per cent and among shipyard workers for only eleven per cent.[2] In 1886 only five of the 95 white-collar City Council officials were Catholics, earning an average salary of £95 per year as against an average salary of £168 for Protestants.[3]

As the Catholic population increased there was a pressing need to provide more churches. Before Bishop Dorrian's death work had begun on St Paul's, a large church on the Falls Road to accommodate those who were moving from the small

1 Report of the commissioners of inquiry, 1864 respecting the magisterial and police jurisdiction, arrangements and establishment of the borough of Belfast . . . minutes of evidence, 75. 2 Hepburn, *A place apart*, 37–40. 3 Ibid., p 124. (Report from the select committee on the Belfast Corporation (Lunatic Asylum etc.) Bill, 1892, (228 – Sess. 1), xi, 323–37, 383–405). Appearing before the select committee inquiring into the Belfast Corporation (Lunatic Asylums etc.) Bill Charles McLorinan claimed that there were ten Catholic doctors and thirty Catholic solicitors in Belfast. James Hamill, the parish priest of Whitehouse, estimated the number of Catholic solicitors as twenty-two or twenty-three and Catholic barristers as four or five.

cramped houses on the Lower Falls. St Peter's Church was no longer able to hold the large numbers at some of the seven Masses celebrated each Sunday. The large cotton mills on the Springfield-Falls district acted as a magnet to workers who wanted to live close by. Bishop Dorrian set aside £4,000, which he had drawn from the revenue of the four churches in the town, to provide the necessary accommodation. Work began in 1884 and was far advanced when the bishop died in November 1885. The riots of 1886 delayed the completion of the building but by July 1887 it was nearly ready for use and because of the pressure of numbers was opened for divine service. By then it had cost £6,300, almost £2,500 of which had been given to Bishop Dorrian by Mrs Coslett of Loughinisland.[4] The solemn dedication took place three months later, on 23 October. Designed to accommodate a congregation of 700, four Masses were celebrated in it each Sunday.[5] The actual collection at the opening amounted to £540 and together with donations made just beforehand a further £1,000 was raised.

Three years later the church of the Sacred Heart was established to provide for the Catholic community on the Oldpark Road. In 1887 a school had been opened in Glenview Street for the children of parents who had moved up mainly from the St Patrick's district, and Mass was celebrated each Sunday in a classroom. The church which cost £2,500 was blessed on 15 June 1890. Fr James Cullen SJ, who preached the special sermon, said it was a memorial to the great movement for temperance, and McAlister, who had long campaigned for temperance, referred to Cullen's connection with devotion to the Sacred Heart through the Apostleship of Prayer.[6] Work began a little later on an adjoining presbytery. Five years later, as appeals were made to pay off the debts, it was reported that the school had increased four-fold in numbers.[7]

4 MN, 1 Oct. 1887.   **5** Curran, *St Paul's, the story of inner West Belfast*, 30–1.   **6** MN, 16 June 1890. Cullen founded the Pioneer Total Abstinance League.   **7** IN, 7 July 1894.

During the 1890s two suburban churches were built to facilitate domestic staff who found it difficult to obtain sufficient free time on Sunday mornings to attend St Malachy's and St Patrick's churches. An oratory was provided in a new parochial house at Derryvolgie Avenue in 1891, and two years later St Brigid's church for a congregation of 350 was opened. The cost was £3,000 and McAlister himself donated the altar. In 1895 the Holy Family Church, a temporary 'zinc' structure, on Newington Avenue was opened a few days before McAlister's death. In 1890 two outlying churches for the parishes of Kilkeel and Lisburn were completed at Attical and Magheragall, and in 1891 a smaller church at Bangor, dating to 1851, was replaced. In 1888 the extensively rebuilt church at Glassdrumman was re-opened. Several parochial houses as residences for the clergy were also built.[8]

Shortly after his appointment McAlister regularized the positions of the parishes of Ballyclare, Greencastle and Holywood. Churches at all three places had been built during William Crolly's episcopate (1825–35). Ballyclare and Greencastle were served directly by the clergy of Belfast, and Holywood, which was attached to Ballymacarrett, formed part of a separate parish. In his reorganization in 1866 Bishop Dorrian took Ballymacarrett into the parish of Belfast, placed it under the charge of an administrator and appointed a parish priest to Holywood. He later made similar appointments to Ballyclare and Greencastle, but neglected to obtain formal authorization from Rome to erect those districts into parishes. For most of McAlister's episcopate there were fifty-three parishes in the diocese, and the parish of Belfast, of which he was parish priest, was divided into seven sub-parishes under the care of administrators.

---

8 In April 1894 a charity sermon was preached at Duneane to pay the debts incurred by the erection of two presbyteries and the enlargement of two cemeteries. (IN, 5 Apr. 1894). Several churches throughout the diocese were renovated. In 1889 Glenravel church was rededicated after extensive repairs. (IC., 26 Oct. 1889)

Six of these administrators were diocesan clergy and the seventh, whose precise role was disputed, was the Passionist who headed the small Passionist community of four priests at Ardoyne. The total number of diocesan priests was 140.

These seven parishes had a total population of about 55,000. St Peter's the largest, which had 18,500 was served by six priests, and St Joseph's, the smallest, which had 2,200 was served by two priests. The ratio of priests to people in St Peter's was 1:3,074 and in St Patrick's, 1:2,903. In the others it was less than 1:2,000. In Belfast the Sisters of Mercy, with thirty-three, had the largest number of nuns; they conducted a school, had charge of the Mater Infirmorum Hospital (the converted Bedeque House) and visited the sick and poor. The nine Bon Secour Sisters did similar social work. The Good Shepherd Sisters and the Sisters of Nazareth, numbering fifteen and six-teen respectively, looked after homeless girls, orphans, the old and sick poor. The twelve Dominican Sisters ran primary and secondary schools on the Falls Road. In Downpatrick there were fifteen Sisters of Mercy, who carried out the same aposto-late as their colleagues in Belfast, and in Lisburn the eleven Sisters of the Sacred Heart of Mary ran both primary and sec-ondary schools. Fourteen Christian Brothers had charge of a thousand pupils in three schools in Belfast, one of which brought boys to secondary level.[9]

McAlister also responded to the social and welfare needs of the expanding industrial city of Belfast. In the year following his appointment he established St Patrick's Roman Catholic Orphan Society, which collected money to make grants to chil-dren or young people who had lost one or two parents but were being cared for by friends or relatives, to cover expenditure on food, clothing and education. The society also undertook to find suitable families to look after children who were left desti-tute or had no relatives or guardians to look after them. Funds

9 Copy of *Relatio Status Dioecesis*, 1888, DCDA.

were raised by annual parish collections, through collecting cards and by bequests. In 1891 the society was responsible for 300 children. The collections in 1892 yielded £1,037 and in 1894 the substantial sum of £1,282 which was disbursed in weekly grants to almost 400 children in their own homes.[10] In 1894 the Society reported that 1,232 orphans had been listed on their books; of these 56 had been adopted and the others had been given weekly grants for fixed periods. At that time nearly 400 were in receipt of grants.[11] In the same year the Belfast Catholic Ladies' Association of Charity undertook to make similar provision for girls.

That association had been set up in 1887. It collected money to provide food and clothing for the sick and poor whose families could not, or, through neglect, did not, care properly for them.[12] In 1889 McAlister encouraged the Sisters of Mercy to found a home for orphaned or indigent girls close to their convent on the Crumlin Road and in April 1890 the St Vincent de Paul Society established a home in Academy Street to provide shelter and food for boys, and to provide needy and hungry boys with meals.[13] Boys aged from seven to fifteen years were admitted, and at the end of its first year the St Vincent de Paul Society reported that it had provided over 20,000 meals, and that more than 5,500 had stayed in the home, of whom 124 were regarded as inmates, as they had stayed for several weeks. The children were sent out to schools and some trained for trades in a workshop, and all were given religious instruction, and employment was found for some of them. Those who could afford to pay the nominal sum of one penny for a night's lodging and the same amount for a day's meals were encouraged to do so. The home was open to all children irrespective of

10 IN, 29 Mar. 1894.   11 Ibid., 26 Mar. 1894.   12 Ibid., 23 Oct. 1891.
13 In supporting the annual collection in 1892 the *Irish News* reported that 300 children were receiving help, partly or wholly from the society and that expenditure of £2,000 was entailed. (IN, 20 Feb. 1892)

religious background.[14] The male and female industrial schools, which for the most part educated children referred to them by court orders, had enrolments of around 250 pupils.

One of McAlister's greatest concerns was the misery – a concern he shared with his episcopal colleagues – caused to families by alcoholism or excessive drinking. In 1888 he founded a Temperance League linked to and supported by the Apostleship of Prayer, which called on those who drank alcohol to make a spiritual sacrifice through temperance, and invited others to support the cause of temperance by their prayers. Within two years he was hopeful that branches of this movement would be established in every parish and school in the diocese.[15] By 1891 there were 31,000 members in the diocese; two years later that figure had risen to 54,498.[16] In his Lenten pastoral letters he repeatedly pleaded for restraint in the use of alcohol as the only means of combating the evils associated with over-indulgence.[17]

However, he did not share some of his brother bishops' views on the weekend closing of public houses. Most of them supported the policy of closing bars at 9.00pm on Saturdays and of extending the *bona fide* clause, which permitted the consumption of alcohol on Sundays only to those who had travelled six miles. When William Johnston of Ballykilbeg, the Orange leader and member of parliament, who was a determined advocate of temperance, accused him of viewing 'efforts to carry the Sunday Closing bill as an insidious attempt to establish a system of legal boycotting' he clarified his position in a letter to the press pointing out that he was not opposed to Sunday closing where it

14 MN., 17 Feb. 1890, 12 May 1891. In the report of 1894 it was stated that 88 boys had been admitted as inmates, employment had been found for 40 boys, 60 were supplied with clothing and six sent to industrial schools. 34,365 meals had been supplied, 8,979 beds had been provided (presumably for very brief accommodation), 440 destitute children were in need of assistance since the last appeal and the committee had taken larger premises at Great George's Street. (IN, 8 Dec. 1894)   15 McAlister to Kirby, 18 Jan. 1890, AICR.   16 IN, 20 Feb. 1893.   17 IN, 29 Feb. 1892, IN, 20 Feb. 1893, IC, 2 Mar. 1895.

would prevent Sunday drinking. He explained that he was opposed 'to establishing a system of legalized boycotting under the name of local option or direct veto'. He then clarified his attitude by reproducing a letter he had written to the Irish Association for the Prevention of Intemperance five years previously. In it he maintained that total Sunday closing often led to illicit drinking in shebeens and, what was worse, drinking at home, in which women and children gradually joined. He also regarded the attempts of the association to include provision in the Sunday Closing Bill 'for the majority of the people of each district to prohibit, by a direct veto, the sale of intoxicating drinks in their localities as an attempt to establish legalized boycotting, and as a death warrant to hundreds of virtuous and respectable Catholic traders in the North of Ireland'. He added that, if the Irish Parliamentary party did not oppose the bill, it deserved to forfeit the confidence of the Catholics of Ulster.[18] The bill was duly passed and provoked little clerical protest, though the Irish Parliamentary party on behalf of the vintners tried to defeat it.

The project to which McAlister devoted his greatest concern was the construction of a new hospital. In 1883 his predecessor, Dorrian, had bought a large residence on the Crumlin Road and invited the Sisters of Mercy to convert it into a hospital. But it was only capable of holding twenty-eight beds and an out-patients' department. With the growth of Belfast and the proportionate decline of hospital places for the population the need to make much better provision for the sick became obvious. McAlister made arrangements with Thomas Drew, the president of the Institute of Architects in Dublin, to judge any plans submitted for a new hospital,[19] and when the president

---

18 IC, 4 Feb. 1893. Supporters of 'local option' regarded it as a first step to nationwide prohibition. 19 IN, 26 Mar. 1894. The paper noted that 37,000 had received treatment in the hospital which was too small for their needs. The new one would have to have 150 beds including those for officers and working staff.

made his choice from the fourteen submitted the bishop called a public meeting to organize a general appeal. Though unwell, he forced himself to attend what became the last public meeting of his episcopate in St Mary's Hall and then explained the need for the undertaking. One speaker pointed out that between five and six thousand people had received treatment in the old hospital during the previous year, and almost 43,000 since its establishment eleven years previously. Anxious to ensure that the hospital would have cross-community backing, as it had already served all denominations equally, McAlister obtained the support of the high sheriff, Henry Jones McCance, and of Samuel Young MP,[20] as well as of prominent Catholics. When the appeal fund was opened it was revealed that the bishop had contributed £2,600, the purchase price of seven houses beside the old hospital which would form the site for the new one. Generous subscriptions of £100, £50 and lesser sums totalled £5,000 for the night, which was thought (mistakenly as it turned out) to account for a quarter of the total cost.[21] At a public meeting McAlister was elected chairman of the executive committee of thirteen clergy and eleven lay people chosen to oversee the construction of the hospital.[22] The Mater Infirmorum Hospital was eventually opened with 150 beds in 1900, five years after the bishop's death.

Apart from the construction of new ecclesiastical buildings, fund-raising during McAlister's episcopate went on apace to liquidate the debts accumulated on extensions and repairs to churches, schools and parochial houses. The two most popular means of collecting money for these purposes were the charity

---

20 In introducing Young, who was about to visit Rome, to Kirby, McAlister described him as a Presbyterian and a very good man who contributed liberally to Catholic churches. He had recently given £20 to the construction of the new St Brigid's church near his home. (McAlister to Kirby, 3 Mar. 1892, AICR) 21 Ibid., 25 Sept. 1894. Mention was made at the meeting of the meagre hospital facilities in Belfast compared to those in Dublin and Cork. In Cork there was one hospital per 7,500 of the population, in Dublin one per 12,000 but in Belfast only one per 26,000. 22 IN, 2 Oct. 1894.

sermon, when a bishop or distinguished preacher was called upon to make an appeal, and the bazaar or sale of work donated or offered at reduced costs for the occasion. In November 1888 a major bazaar was held in St Mary's Hall to pay off debts accumulated in the construction of St Patrick's, St Joseph's and St Paul's churches.[23] To highlight the importance of the bazaar and attract greater support, he sought the assistance of Archbishop Kirby of the Irish College, Rome, requesting him to obtain a gift from the pope which would be a star prize.[24] Kirby succeeded in obtaining a statue blessed by the pope. Almost £5,000 was raised.[25] In the following year a bazaar was held at Lisburn to clear the debts on the church at Magheragall and the hall and parochial house. By 1893 those debts still stood at £11,000 and a charity sermon was preached to help clear them. Extensive work was planned in the parish: the completion of the church at Magheragall, the improvement of the church at Lisburn, the furnishing of the parochial hall and the provision of a cemetery. A school and teacher's residence had been built at Magheragall.[26] Not long before McAlister's death in 1895 a bazaar was held in the Ulster Hall, Belfast to liquidate the debts on St Matthew's parish. A cameo of the Madonna presented by the pope was the top prize on offer.[27]

The pastoral care of the people was augmented frequently by parish missions conducted by members of religious orders. Often lasting two or three weeks[28] the missions afforded opportunities for renewal and re-commitment through the sacraments of penance and the Blessed Eucharist. Masses and confessions punctuated the mornings often from 5.00 a.m. or 6.00 a.m. until 11.00 a.m. or midday, and confessions were again heard in the evenings, when the day's activities concluded with the

23 MN, 20 Nov. 1888. The *Morning News* paid tribute to some Protestant firms which had contributed, and, in particular, to Sir Edward Potter Cowan. 24 McAlister to Kirby, 24 Feb. 1888, AICR. 25 MN, 12 Dec. 1888. 26 IN, 8 Aug. 1893. 27 Ibid., 11 Aug. 1894, 29 Jan. 1895. 28 IN, 2 Oct. 1893.

rosary, a sermon and benediction. In Belfast the missions seem to have been held most years and in the country parishes every two or three years. The response of the people on these occasions seems always to have been high. Very few ignored the mission activities completely. In October 1893 the missions in all the Belfast churches, apart from Ardoyne and the Sacred Heart, lasted four weeks, with morning Masses beginning at 6.00 a.m. or 7.00 a.m. and confessions continuing from then until 2.00 p.m. or 3.00 p.m., and after evening devotions at 6.00 p.m. confessions were heard until 9.00 p.m. or 10.00 p.m. Shorter missions of two or three weeks known as renewal missions were held in the city churches in the following spring.[29] In the country parishes the missions generally lasted two weeks.

The increase of religious devotions and confraternities, like the parish mission, was a consequence of the spreading influence of ultramontanism in the church from the early nineteenth century. Such devotions had been developing in Down and Connor since the 1830s. By the 1880s few parishes did not have a confraternity or sodality or special novenas for the major feasts. Attendance on weekdays proved easier in the town and city parishes. In 1893 an Irish national pilgrimage to Rome was arranged to participate in a jubilee or holy year proclaimed by Leo XIII and McAlister supported the pilgrimage by appealing for associate members to identify themselves with it by the recitation of prescribed prayers.[30]

The *esprit de corps* of parishes in Belfast or of associations or societies within parishes was strengthened by annual excursions to the seaside. Groups led by bands generally marched off to the railway station and on their return marched back to their base. Some Protestant opponents regarded this as a provocation, though political symbols and tunes were excluded, and attacked the processions with fists or stones. Such scuffles occurred in

29 IN, 2 Oct. 1893, 9 Apr. 1894. **30** IN, 9 Jan. 1893.

June and July 1888 and again in 1894. On the latter occasion serious rioting broke out when bands heading groups from St Matthew's and St Joseph's parishes were stoned by Orangemen as they passed through Whitehouse, and, though the police broke up the attacks, five or six people were seriously injured.[31]

In the first half of the nineteenth century, Protestants, especially Presbyterians, subscribed generously to the erection of Catholic churches. In 1815 they contributed a third of the costs of St Patrick's. But with the rise of Fenianism and Home Rule 'ecumenical' relations worsened and such contributions diminished. But they did not disappear. In February 1889 the Catholics of Lisburn expressed their thanks to the firm of William Barbour and Sons for its munificent donation of £100 and noted that it had employed large numbers of Catholics and had always been distinguished by a spirit of liberality and freedom from sectarian bigotry.[32] In 1891 Alex McMullan of Ballymena thanked the Protestants of the town for subscribing to his parish funds and for the kindness he had received from many gentlemen since he came to the town.[33] And Eugene McCartan of Antrim thanked the Protestants of that town for their help in renovating his church.[34] In 1888 a couple of prominent Protestants, Henry McCance and Adam Duffin, assisted at the collection for St Matthew's church.[35]

Towards the end of 1894 McAlister sought permission from Rome to have a coadjutor bishop appointed to the diocese. Asking Archbishop Kirby to help expedite his petition, he explained that he had been ailing for a year and was suffering from incurable cancer.[36] He also begged a blessing from the

---

31 MN, 25 June, 2 July 1888, IN, 7 May 1894. 32 MN, 23 Feb. 1889.
33 Ibid., 29 June 1891. 34 IN, 28 Sept. 1891. 35 NW, 13 Feb. 1888.
36 He appeared in public for the last time a month earlier to lay the foundation stone of the Holy Family church.

pope for his new hospital and for himself as he prepared for death.[37] An operation in the following year was not successful, and he died on 26 March 1895. Two days later Requiem Mass was celebrated in St Patrick's church in Belfast and his remains were brought to Ballycastle where they were interred in the cemetery beside the church which he had built.

The obituary in the *Irish News* was both lengthy and laudatory. Among his many qualities which it singled out for praise was his unassuming and unostentatious manner.[38] That judgement was franked by the *Northern Whig* which remarked that 'he came little before the public save in connection with the duties of his office, which he discharged with great faithfulness and zeal'.[39] McAlister's episcopate lasted only nine years but covered the turbulent events associated with the Home Rule Bills, the worst riots in Belfast in the nineteenth century and the Parnell split. In death he returned to Ballycastle where he had passed more tranquil and less worrisome times.

37 McAlister to Kirby, 19 Nov. 1894, AICR.   38 IN, 27–29 Mar. 1895.
39 NW, 27 Mar. 1895.

Appendix I

In 1888 Bishop Patrick McAlister paid his *ad limina* visit to Rome and presented a report on the state of Down and Connor. The statistics on the population of the parishes in the diocese are taken from that report.

Parish	No. of Catholics	Parish	No. of Catholics
Belfast,		Dunloy	1,828
Holy Cross	2,910	Dunloy	1,828
St Joseph's	2,183	Derriaghy	1,310
St Malachy's	8,065	Glenavy	1,865
St Mary's	5,228	Greencastle	1,882
St Patrick's	14,517	Hollywood	558
St Paul's	5,030	Kilclief	800
St Peter's	18,447	Kilcoo	1,800
Ballymacarrett	4,955	Kilmegan (Castlewellan)	1,710
Ahoghill	919	Kilmore (Crossgar)	1,734
Aghagallon	1,975	Kirkinriola (Ballymena)	3,302
Antrim	1,170	Larne	1,480
Ardkeen (Kircubbin)	1,230	Loughgiel	1,799
Armoy	803	Loughinisland	1,587
Ballee	537	Maghera (Newcastle)	1,143
Ballintoy	454	Upper Mourne (Kilkeel)	4,075
Ballyclare	753	Lower Mourne	2,179
Ballygalget	787	Newtownards	1,268
Ballymoney	1,409	Portglenone	1,330
Blaris (Lisburn)	4,232	Portrush	435
Bright	1,435	Portaferry	1,848

Parish	No. of Catholics	Parish	No. of Catholics
Carnlough & Braid	1,810	Ramoan (Ballycastle)	1,043
Carrickfergus	471	Randalstown	1,931
Coleraine	865	Rasharkin	2,087
Culfeightrim	1,140	Rathlin	297
Cushendall	2,900	Saintfield	1,144
Cushendun	1,309	Saul	1,016
Downpatrick	2,894	Skerry (Glenravel)	1,620
Drumaroad	1,050	Tickmacreevan (Glenarm)	1,735
Duneane	3,385	Tyrella (Dundrum)	1,224
Dunsford (Ardglass)	1,418		

Total 140,314

Appendix II

Each year the diocesan inspector of schools in Down and Connor presented a report to the bishop which not only included comments on the state of religious education in the schools but also gave details of enrolments and attendance. These extracts are taken from the Revd Michael Laverty's report for 1888.

Names of parishes and schools	Total on roll	Non-Catholics on rolls	Average attendance
HOLY CROSS			
Holy Cross Female	135		83.7
Holy Cross Male	135	1	92.6
Ligoniel	194		122.7
Total	464	1	299.0
ST JOSEPH'S			
Earl Street Infant	195		145.0
Earl Street Female	157		111.7
Earl Street Male	130		78.8
Total	482		335.5
ST MALACHY'S			
Eliza Street Male	255		192.0
Oxford Street Christian Brothers' Schools	165		146.0
May Street Female	127		67.0
May Street Male	119	2	70.6

Names of parishes and schools	Total on roll	Non-Catholics on rolls	Average attendance
St Malachy's Convent NS	416		285.0
St Malachy's Convent			
Select	50		
Total	1132	2	760.6
ST MARY'S			
St Mary's Female	219		162.9
St Mary's Male	166		137.4
St Mary's Christian			
Brothers' Schools	328		273.0
Millfield Female	180		107.5
Millfield Male	188		131.0
Total	1081		811.8
ST PAUL'S			
St Catherine's Convent NS	278		196.7
St Catherine's Convent			
Select	45		45.0
Total	323		241.7
ST PATRICK'S			
Glenview Street Female	66		38.0
Glenview Street Male	62		43.0
Hardinge Street Female	150		110.5
Hardinge Street Male	187		142.8
St Patrick's Christian			
Brothers' Schools	324		267.0
St Patrick's Infant	257		134.0
St Patrick's Female	130		102.3
St Patrick's Male	153	1	107.3
St Paul's Convent NS	470		322.0
St Paul's Convent Select	90		75.0
Total	1889	1	1341.9
ST PETER'S			
Canavan Memorial Infant	188		136.6
Canavan Memorial Female	213		172.2
Canavan Memorial Male	357		270.3
Conway Street Female	125		82.4
Conway Street Male	113		67.0

St Brigid's	229		144.3
St Columba's	160	8	111.5
St Peter's Female	439		323.9
St Peter's Male	469		343.3
St Joseph's Female	390		298.8
St Joseph's Male	359		282.2
Total	3042	8	2232.5

INSTITUTIONS

St Patrick's Female Industrial School & Orphanage	153		153.0
St Patrick's Male Industrial School &Orphanage	158		150.0
Nazareth House	100		100.0
Total	411		403.0

Belfast Total	**8824**	**12**	**6426.0**

AGHAGALLON

Derrynaseer Female	67	38.6	
Derrynaseer Male	64	36.7	
Tullyballydonnell	58	12	35.1
Derryclone	72	2	52.7
Brankinstown	5	49.2	
Total	346	14	212.3

AHOGHILL

Watercloney	98	16	43.1

ANTRIM

Antrim Female	66	15	35.8
Antrim Male	90	34	59.3
Tannaghmore	110	68	67.0
Total	266	117	162.1

ARMOY

Breen	62	6	44.5

ARDKEEN (Kircubbin)

Ballycranbeg Female	51	10	35.7
Ballycranbeg Male	63	9	48.0
Total	114	19	83.7

Names of parishes and schools	Total on roll	Non-Catholics on rolls	Average attendance
BALLEE			
Ballycruttle	72	2	57.3
BALLINTOY			
Ballinlea	39	11	20.4
Ballintoy	50	0	28.1
Total	89	11	48.5
BALLYGALGET			
Ballygalget	160	28	104.2
BALLYMACARRETT (St Matthew's)			
Bridge End Female	321	0	182.3
Bridge End Male	289	0	190.6
Lagan Village	162	43	83.6
Total	772	43	456.5
BALLYMONEY			
Ballymoney Infant	74	1	44.5
Ballymoney Female	60	2	42.8
Ballymoney Male	46	0	34.2
Dervock	38	12	30.3
Total	218	15	151.8
BLARIS (LISBURN)			
Chapel Hill Female	71	2	37.0
Chapel Hill Male	124	9	79.3
Reilly's Trench	41	10	31.0
Sacred Heart Convent NS	209	0	144.4
Sacred Heart Convent Select	50	1	
Total	495	22	291.7
BALLYCLARE			
Tyrnog	84	5	50.7
BRIGHT (Killough)			
Killough Female	77	2	51.9
Killough Male	80	4	47.1
St Patrick's Female	57		39.5
St Patrick's Male	66	2	44.7
Total	280	8	183.2

CARNLOUGH & BRAID			
Ballyvaddy	80		44.0
Braid	132	32	59.5
Harphall Female	87		61.0
Harphall Male	65		48.0
Total	364	32	212.5

CARRICKFERGUS			
Minorca Place Female	85	34	53.4
Minorca Place Male	44	11	29.6
Total	129	45	83.0

COLERAINE			
Coleraine Female	93		55.0
Coleraine Male	72		43.1
Total	165		98.1

CULFEIGHTRIN			
Craigfad	72		31.4
Glenshesk	49	2	28.3
Ballyucan	92	4	50.5
Ballyverdock	56	6	31.5
Total	269	12	141.7

CUSHENDALL			
Garron Point	40	8	30.2
Ballyemon	72	4	34.5
Cushendall Female	78		45.6
Cushendall Male	63	2	33.3
Glenann	106		41.6
Glenariff	64		27.0
Kilmore	82	10	39.5
Waterfoot	61	5	39.0
Total	566	29	290.7

CUSHENDUN			
Knocknacarry Female	70	5	39.7
Knocknacarry Male	77	7	42.2
Culrany	65		35.9
Glendun	59	4	38.4
Total	271	16	156.2

Names of parishes and schools	Total on roll	Non-Catholics on rolls	Average attendance
DERRYAGHY			
Hannahstown	113	16	60.9
Ballymacward	84	3	38.0
Total	197	19	98.9
DOWNPATRICK			
Bonecastle	95	31	63.1
John Street Male	100		66.3
Mount St. Patrick's Convent NS	263		189.3
Mount St. Patrick's Convent select	11		11.0
Total	469	31	329.7
DRUMAROAD			
Clanvaraghan	150	35	97.6
Drumaroad	92	9	55.0
Total	242	44	152.6
DUNEANE			
Ballynamullan	46	3	30.0
Gallagh	73		39.4
Gortgill	104		54.8
Millquarter	148	12	88.9
Moneynick	74	3	49.6
Total	445	18	262.7
DUNLOY			
Dunloy Female	67		37.5
Dunloy Male	81		50.0
Total	148		87.5
DUNSFORD (ARDGLASS)			
Ardglass Female	50	3	40.0
Ardglass Male	44		37.2
Dunsford Female	47	1	38.6
Dunsford Male	63	6	42.4
Total	204	10	158.2

Appendix

GLENAVY

Glenavy Female	46		30.2
Glenavy Male	70	1	44.6
Aldergrove	55		29.7
Total	171	1	104.5

GREENCASTLE

Greencastle Female	83		61.9
Greencastle Male	102		73.0
Whiteabbey	104	6	70.0
Total	289	6	204.9

HOLYWOOD

St Patrick's	92		63.1

KILCOO

Ballymoney Female	86	2	49.3
Ballymoney Male	78	2	39.6
Tullyree	119	8	62.1
Total	283	12	151.0

KILKEEL

Attical	197	4	115.2
Dunavan Female	102	6	78.0
Dunavan Male	127	2	76.3
Grange Female	75	5	55.4
Grange Male	135	20	78.9
Total	636	37	403.8

KILCLIEF

Kilclief Female	48	2	33.7
Kilclief Male	73	7	47.2
Total	121	9	80.9

KILMEGAN (CASTLEWELLAN)

Castlewellan Female	55	4	37.1
Castlewellan Male	73	6	54.4
Aughlisnafin	73	20	40.2
Total	201	30	131.7

KILMORE (CROSSGAR)

Kilmore	116	8	84.7

Names of parishes and schools	Total on roll	Non-Catholics on rolls	Average attendance
KIRKINRIOLA (BALLYMENA)			
Ballymena Female	63	2	48.6
Ballymena Male	84		66.8
Broughshane	46	17	30.4
Crebilly	82	15	44.0
Harryville Infant	38		28.4
Harryville Female	60		39.1
Harryville Male	55		25.8
Total	428	34	283.1
LARNE			
North End Female	142		77.4
North End Male	124		86.0
Total	266		163.4
LOUGHGIEL			
Carrowcrinn	64	17	29.3
Corkey	57	17	32.0
Loughgiel Female	54		27.4
Loughgiel Male	61	2	31.2
Magherahoney	80	7	37.0
Total	316	43	156.9
LOUGHINISLAND			
Loughinisland Female	82	3	53.0
Loughinisland Male	99	2	63.0
Total	181	5	116.0
MAGHERA (NEWCASTLE)			
Burren	89	9	51.0
Carnacaville	90	28	51.0
Newcastle	120	57	59.8
Total	299	94	161.8
NEWTOWNARDS			
Ann Street Female	65	4	46.5
Ann Street Male	74	1	52.5
Total	139	5	99.0

PORTAFERRY

Ballyphilip Female	156		108.0
Ballyphilip Male	150		109.9
Total	306		217.9

PORTRUSH

Portrush	43	7	31.4

PORTGLENONE

Gortgole	52	23	27.8
Largy	87	6	50.1
St Mary's	69	2	41.7
Total	208	31	119.6

RAMOAN (BALLYCASTLE)

Ballycastle Infant	83	2	57.3
Ballycastle Female	51	2	32.0
Ballycastle Male	58	0	43.1
Total	192	4	132.4

RANDALSTOWN

Creggan	117	11	67.0
Farrinflough	75	0	39.4
Magheralane	40	12	30.3
Randalstown Female	85	0	54.0
Randalstown Male	76	0	47.5
Total	393	23	238.2

RASHARKIN

Rasharkin	81	0	41.2
Tamlaght	68	5	36.8
St Columba's	75	0	33.6
St Mary's	64	8	35.5
St Peter's	78	0	40.0
Total	366	13	187.1

SAINTFIELD

Carrickmannon	123	56	71.1
Darragh Cross	68	0	39.3
Saintfield	74	19	45.8
Total	265	75	156.2

Names of parishes and schools	Total on roll	Non-Catholics on rolls	Average attendance
ST MARY'S (LOWER MOURNE)			
Ballymartin Female	51	16	33.5
Ballymartin Male	84	36	54.0
Brackney	57	0	29.0
Glassdrumman	84	16	52.9
Moneydara	96	4	60.0
Total	372	72	229.4
SAUL			
Ballintogher	93	2	57.0
SKERRY (GLENRAVEL)			
Glenravel Female	97	10	64.9
Glenravel Male	120	11	74.2
Fisherstown Female	115	10	66.4
Fisherstown Male	102	12	68.0
Total	434	43	273.5
TICKMACREEVAN (GLENARM)			
Sea View (Glenarm)	155	0	104.3
Feystown	41	6	34.3
Loughdoo	56	3	29.8
Total	252	9	168.4
TYRELLA (DUNDRUM)			
Ballykinlar Female	50	1	35.3
Ballykinlar Male	60	4	40.7
Dundrum	109	10	69.6
Total	219	15	145.6

Bibliography

MANUSCRIPT SOURCES

Armagh
Armagh Diocesan Archives
Papers of Cardinal Logue and Bishop O'Donnell of Raphoe

Belfast
Down and Connor Diocesan Archives
Papers of Bishop Patrick McAlister
Public Record Office of Northern Ireland
Applications for aid for national schools

Dublin
Dublin Diocesan Archives
Papers of Archbishop William J. Walsh
Archives of the Passionist Province of St Patrick
Papers relating to Holy Cross, Ardoyne, Belfast

Galway
Galway Diocesan Archives
Minute book of bishops' meetings

Longford
Archives of the diocese of Ardagh and Clonmacnois
Papers of Bishop Bartholomew Woodlock

Rome
Archives of the Sacred Congregation for the Evangelization of Peoples
Correspondence and recommendations of the congregation relating to Ireland
Pontifical Irish College
Correspondence of Archbishop Tobias Kirby

Vatican Archives
Papers of the Secretariat of State relating to Ireland
Papers of Cardinal Mariano Rampolla del Tindaro

Thurles
Papers of Archbishop Thomas William Croke

NEWSPAPERS AND PERIODICALS

Belfast News-Letter	*Northern Whig*
Freeman's Journal	*Pall Mall Gazette*
Irish Catholic	*Ulster Observer*
Irish News	*United Ireland*
Morning News	

PARLIAMENTARY PAPERS AND REPORTS

Reports of the commissioners of national education in Ireland
Fifty-ninth report ..., for the year 1892, [C7124], H.C. 1893–94, xxvii, 265
Sixtieth report ... , for the year 1893, [C 7457], H.C. 1894, xxx, pt ii, 1
Sixty-first report ... , for the year 1894, [C 7796], H.C., 1895, xxix, 1
Sixty-second report ... , for the year 1895, [C 8142]. H.C. 1896, xxviii, 1
Report of the Belfast riots commission, with evidence and appendices, [C 4925] H.C., 1887, xviii, 1
Report of the commissioners of inquiry, 1864, respecting the magisterial and police jurisdiction, arrangements, and establishment of the borough of Belfast, H.C. 1865, [3466], xxviii, !. Minutes of evidence and appendix, H.C. 1865 [3466–1], xviii, 27
Report by one of the commissioners of inquiry, 1886, respecting the origin and circumstances of the riots in Belfast in June, July, August, and September 1886, and the action taken thereon by the authorities; also in regard to the magisterial and police jurisdiction, arrangements, and establishment, for the borough Belfast, [C. 5029] H.C. 1887, xviii, 631
Report from the select committee on the Belfast Corporation (Lunatic Asylums etc.) bill, with the proceedings, evidence, index, H.C.1892, [228-Sess. 1], xi, 253
Hansard's parliamentary debates, 4th series, 1892
Reports of religious examination of Catholic schools in Down and Connor, 1886–95 (Belfast, 1887–96)

PRINTED SECONDARY SOURCES

Akenson, D.H., *The Irish education experiment: the national system of education in the nineteenth century* (London & Toronto, 1970).
Armour, W.S., *Armour of Ballymoney* (London, 1934).
Bardon, J., *A history of Ulster* (Belfast, 1992).

Beckett, J.C., *The making of Modern Ireland* (London, 1966).
Bew, P., *Land and the national question in Ireland, 1858–1882* (Dublin, 1978).
——, *Charles Stewart Parnell* (Dublin, 1980).
——, *Conflict and conciliation in Ireland, 1890–1910: Parnellites and radical agrarians* (Oxford, 1987).
——, *John Redmond* (Dundalk, 1996).
Boyce, D.G., *The Irish question and British politics, 1868–96* (Basingstoke, 1996).
——, *The revolution in Ireland, 1879–1923* (London, 1988).
Buckland, P., *Ulster unionism and the origins of Northern Ireland, 1886–1922,* 2 vols. (Dublin and New York, 1972).
Budge, I., and O'Leary, C., *Belfast: approach to crisis: a study of Belfast politics, 1613–1970* (London, 1973).
Bull, P., *Land, politics & nationalism: a study of the Irish land question* (Dublin, 1996).
Callanan, F., *The Parnell split, 1890–91* (Cork, 1992).
——, F., *T.M. Healy* (Cork, 1996).
Clarke, S., *Social origins of the Irish land war* (Princeton, 1979).
Clarke, S., and Donnelly, J.S. (eds.), *Irish peasants, violence and political unrest, 1780–1914* (Manchester, 1983).
Collins, P., (ed.) *Nationalism and Unionism: conflict in Ireland* (Belfast, 1994).
Comerford, R.V., 'The land war and the politics of distress', in *New history of Ireland, VI: Ireland under the Union,* II, 1870–1921 (Oxford, 1996), pp 26–52.
Comerford, R.V., 'The Parnell era', ibid., pp 53–80.
Connolly, S., *Religion and society in nineteenth century Ireland* (Dundalk, 1985).
Curran, D., *St Paul's: the story of inner West Belfast* (Belfast, 1987).
Curtis, L.P., *Coercion and conciliation in Ireland, 1880–1892: a study of Conservative unionism* (Oxford, 1963).
——, 'One class and class conflict in the Land war', *Irish Economic and Social History,* (1981).
Donnelly, J.S., *Landlord and tenant in nineteenth-century Ireland* (Dublin, 1973).
——, *The land and the people of nineteenth-century Cork: the rural economy and the land question* (London, 1975).
Dugdale, B., *Arthur James Balfour,* 2 vols. (London, 1936).
Egremont, M., *Balfour: a life of Arthur James Balfour* (London, 1980).
Elliott, M., *The Catholics of Ulster: a history* (London, 2000).
English, R., and Walker, G., *Unionism in Modern Ireland* (Basingstoke, 1996).
Foster, R.F., *Lord Randolph Churchill: a political life* (Oxford, 1981).
——, *Modern Ireland, 1600–1972* (London, 1988).
Gailey, A., *Ireland and the death of kindness: the experience of constructive unionism, 1890–1905* (Cork, 1987).

Garvin, T., *Nationalist revolutionaries in Ireland, 1858–1928* (Oxford, 1987)

Geary, L.M., *The Plan of Campaign, 1886–1891* (Cork, 1986).

Gibbon, P., *The origins of Ulster Unionism* (Manchester, 1975).

Hempton, D., and Hill, M., *Evangelical Protestantism in Ulster society, 1740–1890* (London and New York, 1992).

Hepburn, A.C., *A past apart: studies in the history of Catholic Belfast, 1850–1950* (Belfast, 1996).

Hirst, C., *Religion, politics and violence in nineteenth-century Belfast: the Pound and Sandy Row* (Dublin, 2002).

Hoppen, K.T., *Elections, politics and society in Ireland, 1832–1885* (Oxford, 1984).

——, *Ireland since 1800: conflict and conformity* (London, 1989).

Jackson, A., *The Ulster party: Irish unionists in the House of Commons, 1884–1911* (Oxford 1989).

——, *Ireland 1798–1998* (Oxford, 1999).

——, *Colonel Edward Saunderson: land and loyalty in Victorian Ireland* (Oxford, 1995).

Joyce, P.J., *John Healy, archbishop of Tuam* (Dublin, 1931).

Larkin, E., *The Roman Catholic Church and the creation of the modern Irish state, 1878–1886* (Dublin, 1975).

——, *The Roman Catholic Church and the Plan of Campaign in Ireland, 1886–1888* (Cork, 1978).

——, *The Roman Catholic Church in Ireland and the fall of Parnell, 1888–1891* (Liverpool, 1979).

Leslie, S., *Henry Edward Manning* (London, 1921).

Loughlin, J., *Gladstone, Home Rule and the Ulster Question, 1882–1893* (Dublin 1986).

Lyons, F.S.L., *The Irish Parliamentary Party, 1890–1910* (London, 1951).

——, *The fall of Parnell, 1890–1* (London, 1960).

——, *John Dillon: a biography* (London, 1968).

——, *Charles Stewart Parnell* (London, 1977).

——, & Hawkins, R.A.J., *Ireland under the Union: varieties of tension: essays in honour of T.W. Moody* (Oxford, 1980).

Macaulay, A., *Patrick Dorrian, Bishop of Down and Connor, 1865–85* (Dublin, 1987).

——, *The Holy See, British policy and the Plan of Campaign in Ireland* (Dublin, 2002).

MacDonagh, M., *The life of William O'Brien, the Irish nationalist: a biographical study of Irish nationalism, constitutional and revolutionary* (London, 1928).

MacKnight, T., *Ulster as it is* (London, 1896).

Matthew, H.C.G., *Gladstone, 1865–1898* (Oxford, 1995).

McMinn, R.B., *Against the tide: J.B. Armour, Irish Presbyterian minister and Home Ruler* (Belfast, 1985).

Morrissey, T., *William J. Walsh, archbishop of Dublin, 1841–1921* (Dublin, 2000).

——, *Bishop Edward Thomas O'Dwyer of Limerick, 1842–1917* (Dublin, 2003).

O'Brien, C.C., *Parnell and his party, 1880–90* (Oxford, 1964).

O'Callaghan, M., 'Parnellism and crime: constructing a conservative strategy of containment', in D. McCartney (ed.), *Parnell, the politics of power* (Dublin, 1991) pp 102–24.

——, *British high politics and a nationalist Ireland: criminality, land and the law under Forster and Balfour* (Cork, 1994).

O'Day, A., *Irish Home Rule, 1867–1921* (Manchester, 1998).

O'Grada, C., *Ireland: a new economic history, 1780–1939* (Oxford, 1994).

O'Laverty, J., *An historical account of the diocese of Down and Connor, ancient and modern,* 5 vols. (Dublin, 1878–95).

Phoenix, E., 'The history of a newspaper: the Irish News, 1855–1995', in *A century of northern life,* ed. E. Phoenix (Belfast, 1995), pp 12–17

Pomfret, J., *The struggle for land in Ireland, 1800–1923* (Princeton, 1930).

Rafferty, O.P., *Catholicism in Ulster 1603–1983: an interpretative history* (London, 1994).

Roberts, A., *Salisbury: Victorian titan* (London, 1999).

Rogers, P., 'St Malachy's College, Belfast, 1833–1933' in *The Collegian* (1933) 13–29.

Shannon, C.B., *Arthur J. Balfour and Ireland, 1874–1922* (Washington, 1988).

Shannon, R., *Gladstone, heroic minister, 1865–1898* (London, 1999).

Steele, D., *Lord Salisbury: a political biography* (London,1999).

Stewart, A.T.Q., *The narrow ground: patterns of Ulster history* (London, 1977).

Tierney, M., *Croke of Cashel: the life of Archbishop Thomas William Croke, 1823–1902* (Dublin, 1976).

Townshend, C., *Political violence in Ireland: government and resistance since 1848* (Oxford, 1983).

Walker, B.M., *Ulster politics: the formative years* (Belfast, 1989).

Walker, G., *A history of the Ulster Unionist Party: protest, pragmatism and pessisism* (Manchester, 2004).

Walsh, P.F., *William J. Walsh, archbishop of Dublin* (London, 1928).

Ward, J.E., 'Leo XIII, the diplomat pope', in *Review of Politics,* XXVIII (1966), pp 47–61.

Warwick-Haller, S., *William O'Brien and the Irish land war* (Dublin, 1990).

Index